INTRODUCING ISSUES WITH OPPOSING VIEWPOINTS®

Factory Farming

Lauri S. Scherer, *Book Editor*

GREENHAVEN PRESS
A part of Gale, Cengage Learning

GALE
CENGAGE Learning·

Farmington Hills, Mich • San Francisco • New York • Waterville, Maine
Meriden, Conn • Mason, Ohio • Chicago

Patricia Coryell, *Vice President & Publisher, New Products & GVRL*
Douglas Dentino, *Manager, New Products*
Judy Galens, *Acquisitions Editor*

LIBRARY OF CONGRESS CATALOGING-IN-PUBLICATION DATA

Factory farming / Lauri S. Scherer, book editor.
    pages cm. -- (Introducing issues with opposing viewpoints)
Includes bibliographical references and index.
ISBN 978-0-7377-7235-7 (hardcover)
1. Factory farms. I. Scherer, Lauri S., editor. II. Series: Introducing issues with opposing viewpoints.
SF140.L58F333 2015
636--dc23
                                                                    2014041175

Printed in the United States of America
1 2 3 4 5 6 7 19 18 17 16 15

Contents

Foreword

Indulging in a wide spectrum of ideas, beliefs, and perspectives is a critical cornerstone of democracy. After all, it is often debates over differences of opinion, such as whether to legalize abortion, how to treat prisoners, or when to enact the death penalty, that shape our society and drive it forward. Such diversity of thought is frequently regarded as the hallmark of a healthy and civilized culture. As the Reverend Clifford Schutjer of the First Congregational Church in Mansfield, Ohio, declared in a 2001 sermon, "Surrounding oneself with only like-minded people, restricting what we listen to or read only to what we find agreeable is irresponsible. Refusing to entertain doubts once we make up our minds is a subtle but deadly form of arrogance." With this advice in mind, Introducing Issues with Opposing Viewpoints books aim to open readers' minds to the critically divergent views that comprise our world's most important debates.

Introducing Issues with Opposing Viewpoints simplifies for students the enormous and often overwhelming mass of material now available via print and electronic media. Collected in every volume is an array of opinions that captures the essence of a particular controversy or topic. Introducing Issues with Opposing Viewpoints books embody the spirit of nineteenth-century journalist Charles A. Dana's axiom: "Fight for your opinions, but do not believe that they contain the whole truth, or the only truth." Absorbing such contrasting opinions teaches students to analyze the strength of an argument and compare it to its opposition. From this process readers can inform and strengthen their own opinions, or be exposed to new information that will change their minds. Introducing Issues with Opposing Viewpoints is a mosaic of different voices. The authors are statesmen, pundits, academics, journalists, corporations, and ordinary people who have felt compelled to share their experiences and ideas in a public forum. Their words have been collected from newspapers, journals, books, speeches, interviews, and the Internet, the fastest growing body of opinionated material in the world.

Introducing Issues with Opposing Viewpoints shares many of the well-known features of its critically acclaimed parent series, Opposing Viewpoints. The articles are presented in a pro/con format, allowing readers to absorb divergent perspectives side by side. Active reading questions preface each viewpoint, requiring the student to approach the material thoughtfully and carefully. Useful charts, graphs, and cartoons supplement each article. A thorough introduction provides readers with crucial background on an issue. An annotated bibliography points the reader toward articles, books, and websites that contain additional information on the topic. An appendix of organizations to contact contains a wide variety of charities, nonprofit organizations, political groups, and private enterprises that each hold a position on the issue at hand. Finally, a comprehensive index allows readers to locate content quickly and efficiently.

Introducing Issues with Opposing Viewpoints is also significantly different from Opposing Viewpoints. As the series title implies, its presentation will help introduce students to the concept of opposing viewpoints and learn to use this material to aid in critical writing and debate. The series' four-color, accessible format makes the books attractive and inviting to readers of all levels. In addition, each viewpoint has been carefully edited to maximize a reader's understanding of the content. Short but thorough viewpoints capture the essence of an argument. A substantial, thought-provoking essay question placed at the end of each viewpoint asks the student to further investigate the issues raised in the viewpoint, compare and contrast two authors' arguments, or consider how one might go about forming an opinion on the topic at hand. Each viewpoint contains sidebars that include at-a-glance information and handy statistics. A Facts About section located in the back of the book further supplies students with relevant facts and figures.

Following in the tradition of the Opposing Viewpoints series, Greenhaven Press continues to provide readers with invaluable exposure to the controversial issues that shape our world. As John Stuart Mill once wrote: "The only way in which a human being can make some approach to knowing the whole of a subject is by hearing what can be said about it by persons of every variety of opinion and studying all modes in which it can be looked at by every character of mind. No wise man ever acquired his wisdom in any mode but this." It is to this principle that Introducing Issues with Opposing Viewpoints books are dedicated.

Introduction

"We need to be selective about the drugs we use in animals and when we use them. Antimicrobial resistance may not be completely preventable, but we need to do what we can to slow it down."

—William Flynn, deputy director for science policy at the Food and Drug Administration's Center for Veterinary Medicine, December 11, 2013

Few medical discoveries have altered the course of human history as did the advent of antibiotics. Since their discovery in the late nineteenth and early twentieth centuries, these powerful drugs have turned once-debilitating, even fatal illnesses into minor sicknesses that may not even require a missed day of school or work. Only a century after their initial use, however, bacteria are mutating to resist these critical medical weapons, in part because of their widespread use on factory farms.

Antibiotics were first developed to treat diseases in humans but began to be used in the 1950s by large-scale farming operations to treat and prevent disease in animals and soon after, to promote the animals' rapid growth. Their use has become so prominent that sixty years later, the agricultural industry has become the primary market for antibiotics sales. According to Pew Research, 29.9 million pounds of antibiotics were sold in the United States in 2011 just for meat and poultry production; in that same time period, however, only 7.7 million pounds were sold to treat sick Americans. In fact the US Food and Drug Administration (FDA) estimates that a whopping 80 percent of the antibiotics sold in the United States are intended for use in agriculture, mostly for the production of animals for food.

Antibiotics are used by large-scale farming operations (aka factory farms) in two ways. The first is therapeutically, which involves their administration to animals in the event they become sick. This use is widely regarded as justified and is less likely to contribute to antibiotics resistance because doses of antibiotics are given at appropriate levels and for relatively short periods of time to eradicate disease in a specifically targeted group of unhealthy animals.

It is the other use of antibiotics—their nontherapeutic use—that is of much greater concern. *Nontherapeutic antibiotics administration* refers to when an entire flock or herd receives low-level doses over an extended period of time, usually in their food or water, for reasons other than in response to a specific episode of illness. This type of use makes up the bulk of antibiotics use in livestock today. According to the FDA, 74 percent of antibiotics used in livestock are put in feed, and 16 percent in water, for nontherapeutic use; just 3 percent are given via injection to treat illness. "Such widespread use of antibiotics in healthy animals has stimulated the emergence of bacterial strains that are resistant to antibiotics and capable of passing their resistance to human pathogens, many of which can no longer be treated by drugs that were once effective against them,"[1] charge the editors at the *New York Times*. Moreover, mixing antibiotics into livestock's food and water not only makes the animals potential carriers of antibiotic-resistant bacteria but animal waste can spread resistant bacteria into the soil, water supply, and surrounding air, where it can travel far beyond any one particular farm and potentially threaten even those who do not consume the specific animals raised on that farm.

Indeed antibiotics resistance is a looming threat to everyone, not just those who consume factory-farmed products. In 2013 the Centers for Disease Control and Prevention (CDC) looked closely at the growing problem of antibiotics resistance among the general US population. It reported that at least 2 million Americans become infected annually with antibiotic-resistant bacteria; at least 23,000 die from these infections, and many more succumb to other conditions that are made worse by antibiotic-resistant infections. The CDC painted the following dire picture of what could happen should antibiotics resistance worsen:

A simple cut of the finger could lead to a life-threatening infection. Common surgical procedures, such as hip and knee replacements, would be far riskier because of the danger of infection. Dialysis patients could develop untreatable bloodstream infections. Life-saving treatments that suppress immune systems, such as chemotherapy and organ transplants, could potentially cause more harm than good.[2]

The CDC partially blamed this public health threat on factory farmers' inordinate use of antibiotics nontherapeutically in livestock's food and water. The CDC underscored the importance of avoiding such use of antibiotics in livestock farming and using antibiotics "in food-producing animals only under veterinary oversight and only to manage and treat infectious diseases, not to promote growth."[3]

Some argue that the widespread overuse of antibiotics on farms highlights a core problem that undergirds the entire food production system. "Even before getting to the relationship between animal antibiotics and human health, the very need for bulk drugs in factory farms points to the inherent unhealthiness of penning industrial numbers of pigs, cows and chickens in filthy, high-density and stressful conditions,"[4] writes journalist Alexander Zaitchik. Lance Price, an epidemiologist at George Washington University who studies the spread of food-borne illness and bacteria, agrees. "If your production system makes animals sick in a predictable manner, then that system is broken,"[5] asserts Price.

Others, however, claim that the proactive use of antibiotics on livestock populations actually keeps the food supply and the human population safe from disease outbreaks that would be much worse without such use. Industry trade groups such as the National Pork Producers Council argue, for example, that antibiotics keep dangerous diseases out of herds and thus out of the food supply. They also argue that any animals treated with antibiotics must undergo a strict and federally regulated withdrawal period in which antibiotics residue is cleared from their system before they are allowed to go to market.

Finally meat producers claim that contrary to research published by the FDA and the CDC that agricultural enterprises use the bulk of antibiotics, in reality, humans and pets use the bulk of antibiotics—ten times what is used in food animal production. For all of these reasons, the National Pork Producers Council and other such groups claim that they "use antibiotics judiciously," especially because "abusing antibiotics would not benefit farmers, animals or consumers."[6]

At the end of 2013 the FDA thrust this volatile issue further into the spotlight when it enacted new legislation that would prohibit certain uses of antibiotics in cattle, chickens, and pigs that are raised for human consumption. By 2017 the new policy will make it illegal for farmers to use antibiotics to promote growth in animals; producers will also have to get a veterinarian's prescription to use antibiotics preventively in herds. Reaction to the announcement was mixed. Some applauded the policy and claimed it was long overdue; others said it did not go far enough in protecting health or preserving the potency of antibiotics, and still others said it was entirely unwarranted.

To what extent factory farming contributes to antibiotics resistance is just one of the many topics explored in *Introducing Issues with Opposing Viewpoints: Factory Farming.* Carefully selected and well-matched pairs explore whether factory farming is safe, humane, environmentally sound, and necessary to feed a growing population. Thought-provoking questions and essay prompts promote critical thinking on this timely and multifaceted topic.

Notes

1. "The Peril of Antibiotic Use on Farms," *New York Times*, December 21, 2013. www.nytimes.com/2013/12/22/opinion/sunday/the-peril-of-antibiotic-use-on-farms.html?_r=0.
2. Centers for Disease Control and Prevention, *Detect and Protect Against Antibiotic Resistance,* 2013. www.cdc.gov/drugresistance/pdf/AR_Initiative_Fact_Sheet.pdf.
3. Centers for Disease Control and Prevention, *Antibiotic Resistance Trends in the United States,* 2013, p. 36. www.cdc.gov/drugresistance/threat-report-2013/pdf/ar-threats-2013-508.pdf#page=36.
4. Alexander Zaitchik, "Big Ag's Big Lie: Factory Farms, Your Health and the New Politics of Antibiotics," *Salon*, January 12, 2014. www.salon.com/2014/01/12/big_ags_big_lie_factory_farms_your_health_and_the_new_politics_of_antibiotics.
5. Quoted in Zaitchik, "Big Ag's Big Lie."
6. National Pork Producers Council, "Antimicrobials/Antibiotics," 2013. www.nppc.org/issues/animal-health-safety/antimicrobials-antibiotics.

Chapter 1

Is Factory Farming Necessary to Meet the Demand for Food?

Acres of seedlings and commercial chicken houses can be seen at a large-scale farm in South Africa.

Factory Farming Can Meet the World's Demand for Food

Jay Rayner

"We need to ... recognise that farming really is an industry."

In the following viewpoint, Jay Rayner argues that embracing industrial methods of farming will ensure food security. The author examines Britain's decreasing food self-sufficiency. In order to avoid food riots and civil unrest, Rayner believes that the country must reexamine its food production methods. Although the organic and local foods movement has become a trend, the author contends that these have compromised the efficiency of food production. Factory-farmed food is not inherently bad, the author maintains, and producing food on a mass scale is the only way to meet the growing consumer demand. Rayner is a novelist and a restaurant critic for *The Guardian*, a British newspaper.

AS YOU READ, CONSIDER THE FOLLOWING QUESTIONS:
1. How many people died in protests against the increasing cost of bread in Mozambique in 2010, according to the author?
2. According to Rayner, what percentage of its apples does Britain import?
3. British consumers spend what percentage of their wages on grocery shopping, as stated by the author?

You have to go back to 1816 to find a serious British food riot, the year after an Indonesian volcano erupted cancelling summer and blighting the global crop. Today, food riots are what happen in Thailand, Mexico or, as we reported last week [September 2010], Mozambique, where seven people died in protests over a 30% hike in the price of bread. The question is whether the circumstances which led to that murderous bout of civil unrest have any implications for Britain. Too often, we regard ourselves as mere observers and commentators rather than potential participants in the dramas surrounding the complexities of food security. Until a few years ago, this was British government policy. A Cabinet Office document, nicknamed by Tim Lang, professor of food policy at City University, the "leave it to Tesco report", argued that we are a rich developed nation which could buy its way out of any supply crisis on the global market.

But with Russia banning wheat exports until the end of 2011, commodity prices lurching upwards and the United Nations' Food and Agriculture Organisation preparing for an emergency meeting to discuss the crisis, that position looks hopelessly naive. Having spent the past month travelling across Britain investigating the sustainability of our food supply for a new TV show, it's clear to me that we risk replacing a culture of a cheap and plentiful present with one of hyper-expense and scarcity in just a few years' time.

Investing in Food Sustainability

We need to look seriously at how we produce our food and how we eat it. Our self-sufficiency has dropped in the past decade from north of 70% to around 60%, according to official figures. Many experts think it may actually be nearer to just 50%. We import 60% of our

Imported New Zealand apples are for sale in a British supermarket. Some feel that factory farming is the best solution for feeding a mass population and thereby relying less on foods imported from other countries.

vegetables. If this drift continues, we will be left exposed to the sort of events that triggered the riots in Africa. We need to make difficult decisions which a lot of people who regard themselves as serious foodies may find deeply unappetising. And we need to make them fast.

Any consumer of gastroporn [indulgent writing and photos about food] in print, online and on our TV screens would imagine we were already having this debate. Words such as local, seasonal and organic have become a holy trinity. But these are merely lifestyle choices for the affluent middle-classes, a matter of aesthetics, and nothing to do with the real issues. Start in the fruit aisle of your supermarket. The major supermarkets are not inherently evil. On balance, they probably help our lives more than they hinder them, but they only respond to consumer demand and what the consumer demands is not always right.

Look at the bags of perfect fruit, shiny, unblemished, the supermodels of the apple world. They only look like that because of the grading out of fruit which, while perfectly edible, is not comely enough for harried shoppers. In Kent [England] recently, I met David Deme, for decades an apple farmer, who a few years ago decided he had to stop supplying supermarkets because he was being forced to "grade out" 30% to 40% of his fruit. He found this unacceptable and chose to move into a premium market, by making apple juice. Other English apple growers have similar stories to tell.

Which goes some way to explaining why Britain, a country perfectly suited to growing apples, now imports 70% of those we eat. The apple shelves are a global tour, from Chile to South Africa, from New Zealand to China, even as we head into prime British apple season. We will never become self-sufficient in apples, but it is possible to reverse the numbers so that only 30% come from abroad, if we stop being obsessed over the look of the fruit and are prepared to pay more for what we buy, so that fruit farmers could invest in new varieties and the best storage techniques.

FAST FACT

The UN Food and Agriculture Organization estimates that 12.5 percent of the world's population was undernourished between 2010 and 2012.

The Farming Industry Is Losing Its Workforce

Cost is key. In the early 90s, we spent roughly 20% of our wages on our shopping bill. Today, it's nearer 10%, even allowing for recent inflation, and we assume these low prices to be a right. The result is margins for our farmers that are so tight many are giving up. Nowhere is this more obvious than in the dairy industry which is not only shedding farmers every week, but losing its future workforce too, as the traditions of family succession dwindle. Farmers' kids don't want to go into the business and their parents don't want them too, either. A country suited to dairy farming is no longer self-sufficient in milk. We're importing the stuff.

The solution, embracing of the kind of super dairy proposed at Nocton Heath in Lincolnshire, which will house more than 8,000 cows, bedded down indoors on sand, is met with howls of derision because it's not "natural". The dairy farmers I've talked to may take issue with it for the impact it could have on smaller farms, but none

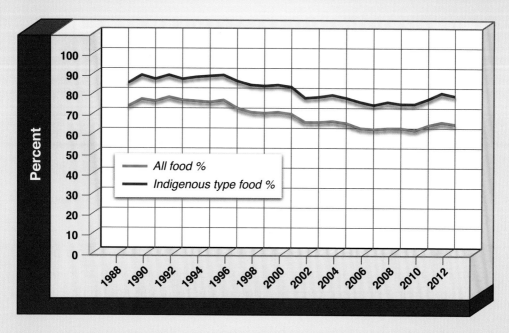

Ratio of Food Production to Supply in Great Britain, 1988–2012

All food %
Indigenous type food %

Taken from: "Agriculture in the United Kingdom," Government of the United Kingdom National Statistics Report, 2012. www.gov.uk.

of them sees animal welfare as an issue. Unhappy, ill animals do not produce milk, so it's not in the farm's interests to mistreat them or shorten their lifespan. Also, the carbon footprint of such a large facility may actually be many times smaller than that of the traditional dairy farm.

Factory Farming Will Ensure Food Security

If we are to survive the coming food security storm, we will have to embrace unashamedly industrial methods of farming. We need to abandon the mythologies around agriculture, which take the wholesome marketing of high-end food brands at face value—farmer in smock, ear of corn, happy pig—and recognise that farming really is an industry, much like car manufacturing or steel forging, one which always works better on a mass scale, but which can still be managed sustainably.

Bespoke is fine for those with deep pockets. As for the rest, we live on a small, overpopulated island with a growing head count and for many big is the only way to go. This is not an endorsement of the worst excesses of the factory farming system. Indeed, only by accepting it can we as consumers get the producers to work to the exacting standards we demand.

Can we afford to ignore these issues? I don't think so. An elitist, belly-obsessed minority, the ones who think the colour plates in the Sunday supplements are a true reflection of real lives if only we all made the effort, may rage against big agriculture and refuse to engage with it. However, when basic ingredients become scarce and prices shoot up on the international markets, their cries will sound increasing hollow, compared to the screams of those who really cannot afford to feed their families. Yes, it has been a very long time since a British food riot, but that does not mean it cannot happen again.

EVALUATING THE AUTHOR'S ARGUMENTS

In this viewpoint, Jay Rayner claims that factory farming is the most effective way to ensure food security. Does his argument convince you to agree with his assertion? Why or why not?

Small-Scale Farms Can Meet the World's Demand for Food

Sian Lewis

"Small-scale sustainable farming could double food production in less than a decade."

In the following viewpoint, Sian Lewis contends that small farms are capable of meeting the global demand for food. The author provides examples of successful small-scale farming systems around the world. She also emphasizes that small-scale farming offers numerous social, economic, and environment advantages compared with industrial farming. Small-scale farming is more efficient, more environmentally friendly, and more likely to provide local jobs, she asserts. Instead of looking at factory farming as the answer to food insecurity, the author argues, societies should support small-scale farms. Lewis is a staff writer for the International Institute for Environment and Development.

AS YOU READ, CONSIDER THE FOLLOWING QUESTIONS:

1. How many small-scale farmers, fishers, and herders in the world are food insecure, according to the author?
2. According to Lewis, how did Kenya build its dairy industry?
3. Why is small-scale farming better at preserving ecosystems, in the author's opinion?

The world's food systems are being squeezed from all sides: rising populations and shifting diets are increasing the global demand for food, while food production is increasingly compromised by climate change and land degradation.

With nearly a billion people already going hungry, how will we manage to feed the world over the coming decades? There's a tendency to suppose that the job will fall to large-scale commercial farmers, who will need to find ways to produce more food, on less land.

But is that right? Are small-scale farmers there to feed themselves and large-scale farmers there to feed the world?

At a 'provocation' seminar held in Stockholm, Sweden earlier this month (3 March 2011), Edith van Walsum from ILEIA [Information Centre for Low-External-Input and Sustainable Agriculture] asked this very question of a room of policymakers, academics and practitioners gathered to discuss how best to support the development of small-scale farmers.

> **FAST FACT**
>
> The International Fund for Agricultural Development estimates that small-scale farmers provide more than 80 percent of the food consumed in sub-Saharan Africa and Asia.

Small-Scale Farmers Can Feed the World

It is true that almost 500 million small-scale farmers, fishers and herders in the world are food insecure. But participants at the seminar were quick to provide a plethora of examples showing that many other small-scale farmers are not only successfully feeding themselves but also wider communities, regions and even whole countries.

Average Size of Agricultural Holdings Around the World

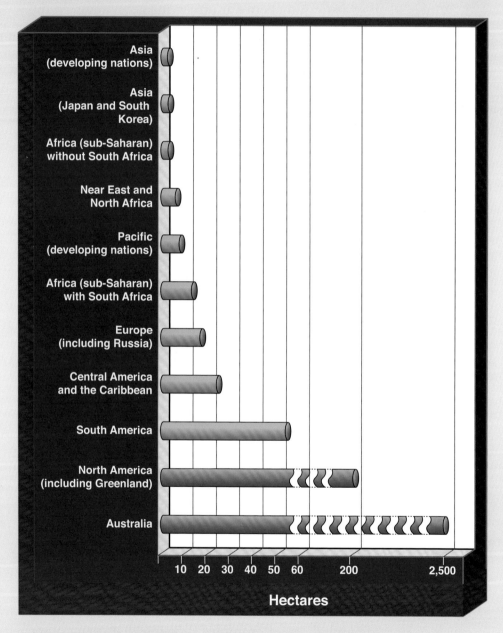

Taken from: "Smallholders and Family Farmers," Food and Agriculture Organization of the United Nations, 2012. www.fao.org.

P.V. Satheesh, founding member of the Deccan Development Society in India, described a network of 5,000 small-scale women farmers in India that is producing food beyond individual households. "Self-sufficiency . . . starts at the farming household—once that household becomes self-sufficient, it starts spreading to the community, local area and then the larger, regional area," explained Satheesh.

In other countries, small-scale producers have been instrumental in supplying entire countries. Katarina Eriksson, from the Tetra Laval group, claimed that Kenya built its whole dairy industry with milk provided by smallholders for school meal programmes. And Kenya is not alone. "Last year, Tetrapak's packages are used in school feeding programmes in 54 countries and in most cases, the milk distributed in schools was locally produced and came from smallholders," said Eriksson.

A similar story can be seen in Brazil, where smallholders play a huge role in supplying food for vulnerable groups, under a food security policy known as Zero Hunger (Fome Zero). Within this programme, the government buys products directly from smallholders at a guaranteed price and distributes them to a network of day-care centres, hospitals and community associations. According to André Gonçalves, from the Centro Ecologico in Brazil, the programme so far involves just 2.5 per cent of the country's small-scale farmers—but their produce reaches a quarter of all food insecure households.

Small-Scale Farming Has Key Advantages

The fact that we already have evidence that small-scale farmers are productive and can contribute to food security is not the only reason for focusing our attention on them. The participants at the Stockholm seminar argued that small-scale farming also offers a number of other key social, economic and environmental advantages.

"Small-scale farming is creating employment and contributing to rural development. . . . It is better at preserving ecosystems because . . . farmers combine various plants, trees and animals on the same piece of land," said speaker Olivier de Schutter, UN special rapporteur on the right to food. "And when the incomes of small farmers increase, it creates a market for services and goods in the country which benefits other sectors of the economy in ways that increased incomes for large landowners do not."

"For all these reasons, it is important to support small-scale farming," he concluded.

Gonçalves agreed, saying that, compared to agribusiness, small-scale farmers are both more efficient and more environmentally friendly. He described a network of more than 3,000 organic farmers in Brazil called the Ecovida Agroecology Network, which exchanges products across regions within the country and is, according to Gonçalves, an 'inspirational' example of how small-scale farming can combine incomes for farmers with environmental services and food production.

Small-Scale Farming Is More Efficient

Last week's [March 2011] report Agroecology and the Right to Food, presented by de Schutter to the UN Human Rights Council, supports Gonçalves's claim that small-scale farming is more efficient, claiming that small-scale sustainable farming could double food production in less than a decade in places where the world's most hungry people live.

Programs such as Brazil's Zero Hunger (shown) utilize local, small-scale farmers to help feed malnourished areas of the country.

In summing up learning from the Stockholm seminar, de Schutter said "there is a largely shared diagnosis at the level of discourse about what needs to be done—switch to supporting small-scale farmers and agroecological methods".

But he added that there are huge obstacles in making this transition, including breaking through the general belief among policymakers that it's all about producing more using the same agro-industrial practices, and ensuring that markets reward small-scale farming. To navigate these hurdles, we need a clearly defined strategy. "We know what the end vision should be but we don't know the itinerary that can lead us there," said de Schutter. He added that the Committee on World Food Security is developing a global strategic framework—"a plan of action for the international community"—over the coming year.

EVALUATING THE AUTHOR'S ARGUMENTS

In this viewpoint, Sian Lewis says that small-scale farmers are productive enough to provide global food security. What reasons can you think of that someone might use to argue that small-scale farms are not equipped to meet the world demand for food?

Support Industrial Slaughter-houses

James McWilliams

"The efficiency of an industrial slaughterhouse . . . is a spectacle to behold."

In the following viewpoint, James McWilliams argues that industrial farming is the most efficient form of food production. He focuses on industrial slaughterhouses and contends that any efforts to localize this industry would be ineffective. Because of the resource-intensive nature of slaughterhouses, McWilliams contends that large-scale operations are the most equipped to handle this industry. Localizing slaughterhouses would be problematic both logistically and environmentally, the author maintains. McWilliams is a professor at Texas State University and the author of *Just Food: Where Locavores Get It Wrong and How We Can Truly Eat Responsibly* and *A Revolution in Eating: How the Quest for Food Shaped America*.

AS YOU READ, CONSIDER THE FOLLOWING QUESTIONS:

1. How long have slaughterhouses been consolidating, according to the author?

2. How, in McWilliams's opinion, do mobile slaughterhouses function?
3. How many federally inspected slaughterhouses are in the United States, as stated by the author?

Last week, on the *New York Times*' Sunday opinion page, Nicolette Hahn Niman, a California rancher who owns BN Ranch with her husband Bill Niman, posed an op-ed kind of question: "When was the last time you saw someone wearing a T-shirt that said 'Support Local Slaughterhouses'?" The answer that immediately popped into my mind was "never, thank God." But Niman was asking the question rhetorically. She thinks it's a great idea.

The first point to note regarding Niman's plea to localize slaughter is that it's essentially self-serving. The pretext to her argument was an

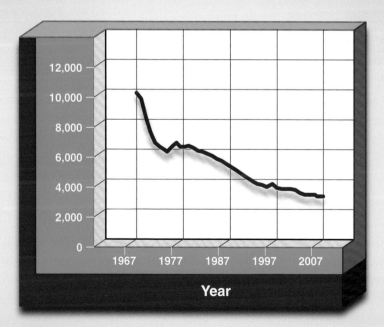

Number of Slaughterhouses in the United States

Taken from: "Meat Atlas: Facts and Figures About the Animals We Eat," Heinrich Böll Foundation and Friends of the Earth Europe, January 2014. www.foeeurope.org.

8.7 million pound beef recall by the Rancho Feeding Corporation, a Bay Area slaughterhouse with whom Bill Niman has worked for over 40 years. The U.S. Department of Agriculture's decision to recall Rancho's meat prevents BN Ranch from selling over 100,000 pounds of its own frozen supply of grass-fed beef. That's unfortunate for the ranch. But the subsequent call to localize slaughterhouses—which have been consolidating since the 1970s—should give the rest of us pause.

Obvious statement alert: Slaughterhouses are nasty and resource-intensive operations. Any hope that they'll become less nasty or resource intensive if scaled down and dispersed is belied by the use of mobile slaughterhouse units (MSUs). Mobile slaughterhouses are currently beloved by locavore-carnivores as a USDA-inspected alternative to industrial-scale operations. MSUs drive to the farm, kill and process a handful of animals on location, provide a USDA stamp of approval, and then trundle off, leaving behind a happy local farmer and cuts of meat he can now legally sell to conscientious carnivores willing to spend more for "humane" meat. No more hacking a cow into quarters and selling them to that eccentric woodsman with a deep freeze.

But small slaughterhouses also leave behind a mass of viscera—namely plasma-flecked wastewater, blood, and offal. In rule-abiding industrial slaughterhouses, these byproducts are effectively disposed of and processed. The efficiency of an industrial slaughterhouse, macabre as it may be, is a spectacle to behold. A farm animal entering the front door will reach the exit about 19 minutes later. It will do so not only as chops destined for the meat counter, but as pelts bound for Turkey, lungs sent to dog-treat manufacturers, bile for the pharmaceutical industry, caul fat (the lining of organs) for Native American communities, and liver destined for Saudi Arabia (which, go figure, distributes cow liver globally).

As MSUs demonstrate, smaller slaughterhouses are much less capable of processing or recycling these organic byproducts. Even if they could, their decentralization would, from a distribution perspective, pose a thorny logistical problem. Example: Large slaughterhouses are critical to the trade in animal blood, which is transformed into blood meal for animal feed. Dispersed slaughterhouses would make it economically prohibitive to collect and recycle this industrial byproduct. Because of their scale, mobile slaughterhouses are authorized to leave

Proponents say that industrial-scale slaughterhouses are able to handle the production of animals much more efficiently than small-scale farms and can also make better use of the entire animal for various products.

behind a literal bloody mess after a day on the farm. Eight slaughtered cows—a plausible number for a small-scale rancher to slaughter with an MSU—generate about 800 pounds of blood. Current USDA rules on what to do with it are less than assuring.

"Blood and waste water might be dispersed on the producer's property," according to the USDA's Food Safety and Inspection Service (FSIS). This dispersal should happen "well away from any stream or drainage." There is no oversight, but it suggests, "Bleeding animals on a sloped concrete pad equipped with lines to a drain field is recommended." And when it comes to the viscera, "farmers can make their own arrangement." The decentralization of slaughter might make it easier for small farmers to kill their animals. But fragmenting the process disperses the blood and guts of slaughtered creatures across the landscape rather than consolidating it in places that are, for good reason, located in the middle of nowhere.

Well, middle of nowhere for you and me. There are about 1,100 federally inspected slaughterhouses in the United States. Each of them exists in someone's backyard. But someone is not everyone. Here's a haphazardly chosen short list of places that have a slaughterhouse in their town limits: Tuscumbia, Alabama; Moscow, Idaho; Boscawan, New Hampshire; Ladonia, Texas; and El Rito, New Mexico. . . .

FAST FACT

There were 1,627 federally inspected slaughterhouses in the United States in 1980, according to the *Washington Post*. By 2010, there were under 1,100.

Aside from housing an abattoir, these towns share other similarities. They typically have household median incomes far below national and state averages, a sparse population, comparatively low property values, and an undereducated workforce. San Francisco, California, lacks a slaughterhouse; so does Brooklyn Heights, New York; Charlottesville, Virginia; and Chapel Hill, North Carolina. (Search "slaughterhouse and Chapel Hill" and you're likely to get hit with a lot of Vonnegut.) It seems safe to predict that even as small-scale animal farming proliferates in these well-to-do areas, slaughterhouses will be kept at bay. All of which raises an interesting follow up question to Niman's proposition: In whose backyards will local slaughterhouses live?

Not Brooklyn's. When the borough's Columbia Street Waterfront District began to gentrify, the lone local slaughterhouse—Yeung Sun Live Poultry—came under heavy fire as a noxious nuisance that sent blood and feathers into the streets. Neighbors complained of escaped animals running around the area, cowering in traffic. Upwardly mobile residents were, according to a 2011 *Times* story on the feud, "too posh for poultry." The reaction was hardly new. The area once hosted three slaughterhouses, but complaints reached a crescendo a decade ago, with a district manager receiving from an angry resident a jar of slaughterhouse ooze that had pooled in the street. When the Yeung Sun Live Poultry was accidentally felled in 2011 by city workers digging a tunnel, residents reacted with a sigh of relief.

Recent research on the long-term impact of slaughterhouses on local communities suggests that the blood and guts aren't the only reason communities will continue to say no thanks to the prospect of a new slaughter facility. It's unlikely that local slaughterhouses will mean more local jobs. The small farmers who are leading a revival of family farming in the United States are generally not the sort of folk who will take a position in the local slaughterhouse. People who work the slaughterhouse floor are the most socioeconomically marginalized and politically disenfranchised people working in North America. Annual turnover rates are often higher than 100 percent. It's one of the most dangerous jobs on the face of the Earth. And, as new research is showing, it leads to crime.

Dr. Amy Fitzgerald, a criminologist at the University of Windsor, draws a disturbing and data-driven conclusion between slaughter-houses and local crime. Analyzing slaughterhouses in 581 counties over eight years, Fitzgerald crunched the numbers to conclude that "slaughterhouse employment increases total arrest rates, arrests for violent crimes, arrests for rape, and arrests for other sex offenses in comparison with other industries." Why would slaughterhouses have a greater impact on local crime than other industries? In talking to *The Toronto Star*, Fitzgerald linked the connection to the act of slaughter. She said of slaughterhouse workers, "One of (the explanations) is the violence they witness and sometimes have to participate in might result in some kind of desensitization." When's the last time you saw a T-shirt saying "Support Local Crime Increase"?

Perhaps the strangest aspect about the call to localize slaughter-houses is that it's being made this late in the game, at least a genera-tion after the backlash against factory farming inspired a shift toward smaller-scale animal agriculture. In a sense, the key question—how can animals raised under alternative conditions be slaughtered under alternative conditions—should have been the first order of business among those seeking to reform the industrial food system. At the same time, it's understandable that this question has been put off as long as it has. There's no way, after all, to avoid the fact that the proposal bangs right into a hard conundrum: People might want local meat but—because that meat requires the violent death of an animal that didn't want to die—they will always prefer that death takes place in someone else's backyard.

EVALUATING THE AUTHOR'S ARGUMENTS

In this viewpoint, James McWilliams claims that large-scale operations such as slaughterhouses are the most efficient forms of food production. On the basis of what you have read, do you think localizing slaughterhouses would benefit the food industry? Why or why not?

Factory Farming Is Not Efficient

Daniel Imhoff and Douglas Tompkins

"High productivity . . . should not be confused with efficiency."

In the following viewpoint, Daniel Imhoff and Douglas Tompkins argue that industrial farming is not the most efficient method of food production. It is a myth that "bigger is better" when it comes to factory farming, they contend. While industrial farming has high productivity, the authors maintain that productivity does not equal efficiency. Hidden in the high productivity numbers of large-scale farming is the detrimental impact of government subsidies as well as the environmental and public health costs. Imhoff is the publisher of Watershed Media and the author of *Food Fight*, *Farming with the Wild*, and *Paper or Plastic*. Tompkins is a wilderness advocate, environmental activist, and the founder of the Foundation for Deep Ecology, which supports grassroots, nongovernmental environmental organizations.

AS YOU READ, CONSIDER THE FOLLOWING QUESTIONS:
1. According to the authors, what do concentrated animal feeding operations rely on to produce feed?

Daniel Imhoff and Douglas Tompkins, "Myth: Industrial Food Is Efficient," *CAFO: The Tragedy of Industrial Animal Factories* (blog), 2013. www.cafothebook.org. Copyright © 2013 Daniel Imhoff and Douglas Tompkins. All rights reserved. Reprinted with permission.

2. What are the hidden costs of confinement operations, as stated by Imhoff and Tompkins?
3. According to the authors, what substitutions allow animal factory farms to achieve their efficiencies?

Industrial food animal producers often proclaim that "bigger is better," ridiculing the "inefficiency" of small- or medium-size farms using low-impact technologies. CAFO [concentrated animal feeding operations], however, currently rely on heavily subsidized agriculture to produce feed, large infusions of capital to dominate markets, and lax enforcement of regulations to deal with waste disposal. Perverse incentives and market controls leverage an unfair competitive advantage over smaller producers and cloud a more holistic view of efficiency.

High Productivity Does Not Equal Efficiency

Factory farms and CAFOs appear efficient only if we focus on the quantity of meat, milk, or eggs produced from each animal over a given period of time. But high productivity or domination of market share should not be confused with efficiency. When we measure the total cost per unit of production, or even the net profit per animal, a more sobering picture emerges. Confinement operations come with a heavy toll of external costs—inefficiencies that extend beyond the CAFO or feedlot. These hidden costs include subsidized grain discounts, unhealthy market control, depleted aquifers, polluted air and waterways, and concentrated surpluses of toxic feces and urine. The massive global acreage of monocrops that produce the corn, soybeans, and hay to feed livestock in confinement could arguably be more efficiently managed as smaller, diversified farms and pasture operations, along with protected wildlands.

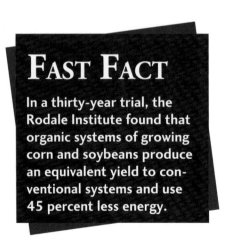

FAST FACT

In a thirty-year trial, the Rodale Institute found that organic systems of growing corn and soybeans produce an equivalent yield to conventional systems and use 45 percent less energy.

Reverse Protein Factories

Animal factory farms achieve their efficiencies by substituting corn and soybeans and even wild fish for pasture grazing. To gain a pound of body weight, a broiler chicken must eat an average of 2.3 pounds of feed. Hogs convert 5.9 pounds of feed into a pound of pork. Cattle require 13 pounds of feed per pound of beef, though some estimates range much higher. To supplement that feed, one-third of the world's ocean fish catch is ground up and added to rations for hogs, broiler chickens, and farmed fish. The 2006 United Nations Food and Agriculture Organization report *Livestock's Long Shadow* summed

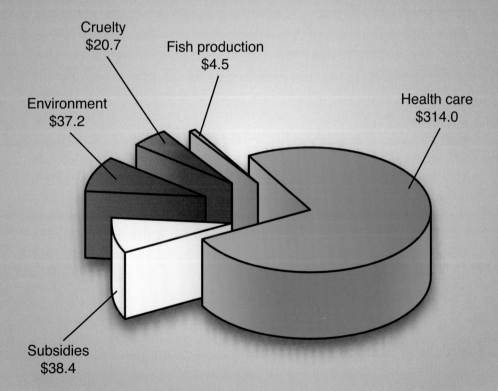

Total Externalized Costs of US Animal Food Production

In US$ billions

Cruelty
$20.7

Fish production
$4.5

Environment
$37.2

Health care
$314.0

Subsidies
$38.4

Taken from: David Robinson, "A New Look at the Strange Economics of Meat and Dairy Production," Meatonomics.com, June 24, 2013. http://meatonomics.com.

it up this way: "In simple numeric terms, livestock actually detract more from total food supply than they provide. . . . In fact, livestock consume 77 million tons of protein contained in feedstuff that could potentially be used for human nutrition, whereas 58 million tons of protein are contained in food products that livestock supply."

Contaminated Food

The efficiency of slaughterhouse practices should also be called into question, as their incessant increases in speed, drive for profit, and huge scale have resulted in contamination and massive meat recalls. In the United States, between spring 2007 and spring 2009 alone, there were twenty-five recalls due to the virulent *E. coli* O157:H7 pathogen involving 44 million pounds of beef. When all costs of research, prevention, and market losses are added up, over the last decade *E. coli* contamination has cost the beef industry an estimated $1.9 billion.

Mounting Waste

The U.S. Department of Agriculture estimates that factory animal farms generate more than 500 million tons of waste per year—more than three times the amount produced by the country's human population. On a small, diversified farm, much of this manure could be efficiently used for fertilizer. Instead, most CAFOs store waste in massive lagoons or dry waste piles with the potential to give off toxic fumes, leak, or overflow. Ground and surface water can be contaminated with bacteria and antibiotics; pesticides and hormones containing endocrine disruptors; or dangerously high levels of nitrogen, phosphorus, and other nutrients. Inconsistent enforcement of regulations has allowed CAFO waste disposal problems to escalate in many areas. Meanwhile, the environmental and health impacts of this pollution are rarely calculated as part of the narrow range of parameters that CAFO operators use to define efficiency.

Government Subsidies

Not only do CAFOs burden citizens with environmental and health costs, they also gorge themselves at the proverbial public trough.

Thanks to U.S. government subsidies, between 1997 and 2005, factory farms saved an estimated $3.9 billion per year because they were able to purchase corn and soybeans at prices below what it cost to grow the crops. Without these feed discounts, amounting to a 5 to 15 percent reduction in operating costs, it is unlikely that many of these industrial factory farms could remain profitable. By contrast, many small farms that produce much of their own forage receive no government money. Yet they are expected somehow to match the efficiency claims of the large, subsidized megafactory farms. On this uneven playing field, CAFOs may falsely appear to "outcompete" their smaller, diversified counterparts.

Lack of Competition

Another issue clouding any meaningful discussions of efficiency is the lack of access to markets among many independent producers. Because CAFOs have direct relationships with meat packers (and are sometimes owned by them, or "vertically integrated"), they have preferred access to the decreasing number of slaughterhouses and distribution channels to process and market products. Many midsize or smaller independent producers have no such access and as a result must get big, develop separate distribution channels, or simply disappear.

> **EVALUATING THE AUTHORS' ARGUMENTS**
>
> In this viewpoint, Daniel Imhoff and Douglas Tompkins claim that industrial farming is not an efficient form of food production. Whose argument is more convincing, these authors' or James McWilliams's? Why? Use evidence from the texts in your answer.

Chapter 2

Is Factory Farming Humane?

Butchers in safety gear work at an Argentinian subsidiary of JBS S.A., the largest food processing company in the world.

Viewpoint

1

Factory Farmed Animals Are Horrifically Mistreated

Leah Garces

"It is a sea of chickens ... sitting in their own feces, struggling to move."

In the following viewpoint, Leah Garces argues that the brutality of the factory farming industry in the United States is horrific. The author highlights issues of animal overcrowding, filthy living conditions, and the spread of disease inside factory farms. Garces contends that the agricultural industry has fought to close off factory farms from the public in order to hide the horrific conditions inside. The author believes that the government must enact meaningful reform and stop protecting the factory farms. Garces is a contributing writer for *Food Safety News*, a member of the board of directors for the Global Animal Partnership, and the USA director for Compassion in World Farming.

AS YOU READ, CONSIDER THE FOLLOWING QUESTIONS:

1. According to the author, which country is the largest producer of chickens?

2. If humans grew as fast as a factory farmed chickens, how much would they weigh at age two, according to the University of Arkansas Division of Agriculture, cited by Garces?
3. What are "ag-gag" laws, as described by the author?

In 2003, the animal protection group Compassion Over Killing produced a video exposé of the biggest farm animal industry in our country—the factory farming of chickens raised for meat. Entitled *45 Days*, it laid out the short, brutal life of a broiler (i.e. meat) chicken: panting, overcrowded, lame, limping and even dead birds. The film shows a bird trapped in a feeder unable to reach water, birds

States with Ag-Gag Laws

Passed   Pending   Failed

Taken from: Ted Genoways, "Gagged by Big Ag," *Mother Jones*, July–August 2013. www.motherjones.com.

in filthy, dusty conditions, and birds with chests so heavy that they were unable to move around with ease.

New Yorker writer Michael Specter wrote separately in 2003 on his first visit to a broiler factory farm, "I was almost knocked to the ground by the overpowering smell of feces and ammonia [from urine]. My eyes burned and so did my lungs, and I could neither see nor breathe. . . . There must have been thirty thousand chickens sitting silently on the floor in front of me. They didn't move, didn't cluck. They were almost like statues of chickens, living in nearly total darkness, and they would spend every minute of their six-week lives that way."

That was nearly ten years ago [in 2003] and still remains the last time the public saw in any detail the life of a factory farmed broiler chicken in the U.S.

Globally, the world raises and slaughters some 40 billion chickens for meat every year—9 billion of whom are right here in the U.S. We are the world's largest producer. More than 99 percent of U.S. broiler chickens are raised in barren windowless enclosed long houses, houses that remain inaccessible to anyone outside the industry.

The Inside of a Factory Farm

Recently in rural north Georgia and south Kentucky, I drove past row upon row of uniform structures—500 feet long, 40 feet wide and windowless—on otherwise barren properties, surrounded often by beige fields of soy and maize. What hides behind the walls?

What starts off as a seemingly spacious, clean (though barren and dimly lit) environment, soon changes. A full 25,000 individual animals defecate in the same enclosed space for 45 days. They get a lot bigger, rapidly growing from the size of your fist to the size of a soccer ball in that short period. They crowd that space as they grow, with each individual only having space equivalent to less than a piece of 8"×11" paper. It is a sea of chickens from wall to wall, sitting in their own feces, struggling to move, in large part because of their genetics. The modern broiler chicken is unnaturally large and has been bred to grow at a fast rate. This selective breeding produces as side effects serious welfare consequences including leg disorders: skeletal, developmental and degenerative diseases, heart and lung problems, breathing difficulty, and premature death. The University of Arkansas Division of Agriculture explains the unnaturally fast growth rate as follows: "If you grew as fast as a chicken, you'd weigh 349 pounds at age 2." They are forced to breathe ammonia and dust filled air, and have no natural lighting.

Most photos and video from factory farms come from undercover investigators who manage to get hired to work within the farm and then secretly gather images for an external organization. This is next to impossible in a broiler factory farm. There is hardly a "job" involved in raising broilers in factory farms anymore. Often there are only one or two people, usually the farm owners, overseeing multiple houses, each house filled with tens of thousands of birds.

Chickens are put into a long windowless structures soon after hatching. They grow in that house and the main job of the farm owner is to remove, dispose of and record the dead birds on a daily basis. A University of Georgia's College of Agriculture and Environmental Science (CAES) study refers to a typical flock of 25,000 birds in Georgia with a 3% mortality rate over 6 weeks. On average, that means 750 birds dying over the 6 weeks in each house and the farmer on average picking up 18 dead birds a day in each house over the 6 weeks. That is the main job—recognizing dead or dying birds, killing sick birds, picking up dead birds and disposing of them. The feed, water and temperature are automated and the litter is never changed during those birds' short life. The job is done easily by one or two people and the farmworker (including a covert one) is hardly required.

An Open Farm Door Policy

But not all farmers are afraid to show off their farms. White Oak Pasture's (WOP) Will Harris raises over a quarter of a million chickens on pasture every year. One can drive along Harris' farm in Bluffton,

GA any time of the day or night and see exactly how the chickens are living—in the fields, in the trees, in the shrubs. He and his daughter Jenni will greet you with pride and eagerness to share their farm and welcome you to take photos of the birds. They have half a dozen certifications hung on the farm office wall showing that they are following the nation's top guidelines for caring for animals.

"Animals were born with certain predetermined instinctive behaviors. So often through the industrialized meat production system, we don't allow that. We believe the way we raise our animals is much better in terms of animal welfare, environmental sustainability and economic impact," says Harris. "I believe good animal welfare means me as the stockman creating an environment that allows the animals to express their instinctive behavior. And the way to know if you are successful is—do you enjoy watching the animals?"

WOP operates with an open farm door policy because they know the image (i.e. watching the animals) is their greatest asset. They are images we think of when we think of "farm"—green pastures, animals roaming, and a farming family as stewards of the animals and the land.

Most Factory Farms Are Closed Off from the Public

This is the challenge that we are faced with today, ten years on from *45 Days*. Dare to be honest about who you are, and you are shown off the property of a large scale broiler farm. Scour the law to find a risk free way of getting unbiased, unedited images and you are faced with laws like the Federal Animal Enterprise Terrorism Act or the Animal Facilities Protection Act. These are laws designed to potentially make it a criminal felony to enter animal rearing properties under false pretenses. There is often little or no case history in many of these states related to factory farms challenging these laws. With no case history, the interpretation of the law remains unclear until someone rolls the dice.

These laws existed before the new so called "ag-gag" laws, which make it illegal to film or photograph a factory farm. The surge of proposed ag-gag laws are a sign of the industry's concern of what might be revealed from within the walls of the factory farm and what impact these revelations might have. Three states—Iowa, Missouri and Utah—have passed these "ag-gag" laws to date. This is a desperate

A wheelbarrow of dead chickens can be seen among living birds in an industrial chicken farm. Such chickens live out their entire lives—approximately six weeks—in a windowless shed, packed together with thousands of other chickens.

reaction by an industry whose worst enemy is the images from within. This fall [2012], for example, Pennsylvania became the latest in a slew of states to propose, and fail to pass, an "ag-gag" law. The senator who introduced the bill was Lancaster County–based Republican Mike Brubaker. He represents Manheim, PA, where the Humane Society of the United States recently conducted an investigation of Kreider Egg Farms. The images from the investigation revealed mummified dead birds crowded in with live birds in tiny cages, thirsty and filthy birds, among other horrors.

This is what our nation's biggest farm animal industry lacks—images that are an asset rather than a liability. It has been nearly ten years since we have seen detailed, unedited images of the short life of a factory-farmed broiler chicken. As consumers become more and more aware of where their food comes from, the broiler industry will have to face that they cannot hide beyond the factory farm walls forever.

At the end of this month [January 2013], the International Poultry Expo in Atlanta will bring together the world's poultry industry. The challenge to this gathering is to stop responding with knee-jerk reactions like "ag-gag" laws and start thinking about meaningful reform, so they aren't so scared of the public seeing what their industry looks like. Key issues like the welfare problems caused by the fast growing breeds, the overcrowding, the barren environment, and the lack of natural light will need to be recognized and addressed. How will we know we have arrived at meaningful reform? We will have arrived when the inside of the chicken farm is not left to our imagination, when there is nothing left to hide.

EVALUATING THE AUTHOR'S ARGUMENTS

In this viewpoint, Leah Garces claims that the agricultural industry keeps factory farms closed from the public to hide their mistreatment of animals. What other reasons might someone use to argue that factory farms should not be open to the public?

Factory Farmed Animals Are Not Mistreated

Jason Smith

"The very largest farms are also the farms with the healthiest, most looked-after live-stock."

In the following viewpoint, Jason Smith contends that animals in large-scale farming operations are not treated worse than those in small-scale farms. In contrast, the author argues, small-farm animals are more likely to have diseases and to produce substandard meat. Small-scale farmers have less capacity to implement new technology and research, Smith asserts, which impacts the quality of their meat production. He believes that factory farms are more efficient, able to implement new technologies on a mass scale, and able to implement operational methods that ensure the welfare of their animals. Factory farming is the future of food production, Smith says, and society needs to address the prejudices against it.

Smith is a columnist at *The Free Society* and founder of the Birmingham Salon, a British debate forum.

AS YOU READ, CONSIDER THE FOLLOWING QUESTIONS:

1. According to the Campaign Against Factory Farming Operations, as quoted by Smith, what will result from an increase in factory farming?

2. Why are small farmers less likely to benefit from new developments in the agriculture industry, as stated by the author?
3. According to Smith, why are most dairy farms in the United States required to develop nutrient management plans?

I wrote an article some months ago on *Spiked* about a campaign against a super-dairy planned for Nocton in Lincolnshire [England]. A planning proposal for an 8,100-cow operation at Nocton Dairies was being considered by North Kesteven District Council. A campaign against the proposals was also getting under way, initially started by Compassion in World Farming (CIWF) and local residents who didn't feel included in the decision making process. Conservationist Bill Oddie, comedienne Jo Brand and actor William Roache (*Coronation Street*'s Ken Barlow) had signed up against the scheme.

Since then the plan for Nocton has diminished in ambition and scale and now plans facilities for 3,770 dairy cows, an 80-cow milking parlour, and special care, maternity and isolation units. While this would still make it the biggest and most efficient dairy farm in the UK, the downscaling of the plans is an example of how today's environmentalist groups hold back developments in the farming industry from which we would all otherwise benefit.

> **FAST FACT**
>
> Dairy farms with more than seven hundred head of dairy cattle are classified by the US Environmental Protection Agency as large concentrated animal feeding operations, or CAFOs, which are subject to special regulations.

CIWF's campaign manager Pat Thomas said: "Every child knows cows belong in fields. Hundreds of residents objected to the initial plans for a 'mega-dairy' earlier this year [2011], but now that a resubmission of the plans is imminent, Compassion is encouraging the local communities to, once again, do all they can to contest the plans. . . . If this huge dairy gets the go-ahead, there would be more cows kept indoors for most of their lives. . . . It would also open the floodgates for similar factory farms all over the country".

Cows are milked at a modern dairy farm. Proponents say that factory farms have the financial resources to purchase the latest technology, keep equipment updated, employ workers to maintain safety standards, and undertake other measures that keep the animals in good care.

The group Campaign Against Factory Farming Operations (CAFFO) says of large specialist farms, these "specialist unit(s) would be 'specialist' in nothing but inflicting an unprecedented amount of agony on thousands of animals at a time. Factory farming animals on this scale will guarantee nothing but a massive rise in levels of disease, infection and injury".

Factory Farms Are More Efficient

While it is true that the amount of time a farmer has to be concerned about the welfare of cattle is linked to how intensively he farms, it is the intensive farmer who is best able to prioritise welfare. The subsistence farmer in Africa is so caught up in the trials of everyday survival that mostly he is unable to look after his own wellbeing. His animals are more likely to be diseased, produce sub-standard meat and less-nutritious milk.

A standard size British dairy farm with around 120 cattle will [fare] much better. The farmer can look after the herd because it is small enough an operation for him to notice any problems with individual cows, even if the herd is mostly a one-man operation. However, financially he is unable to invest in the latest technology. He cannot grow his herd because that would require more labour to handle them. His business is less able to take advantage of efficiency savings because his turnover is too low. Vets' fees are a big concern for him and like any frugal businessman, he must limit such expensive utility bills.

By contrast the factory farm has dedicated full-time vets, is able to benefit from the latest scientific research and can become ever more efficient in its operations. The larger the farm the more developed the division of labour; having specialist slurry removal and housing managers, for instance. This means that animal welfare is planned and organised on an industrial scale. There is much less room for unexpected problems occurring because looking after the health of the animals is built into the farm's operation to a degree unimaginable by the subsistence farmer in Africa. The amount of specialist knowledge and research available to farmers increases as the size of their operation increases. The very largest farms are also the farms with the healthiest, most looked-after livestock.

Most Farmers Consider Super Dairies Acceptable

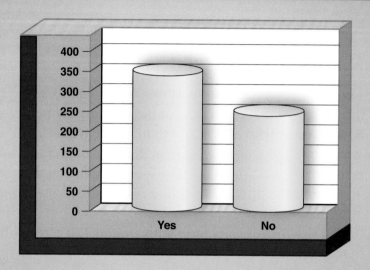

Do you think super dairies, where thousands of cows are permanently housed, are acceptable?

Note: Data from survey of more than 600 dairy farmers at the 2010 Dairy Event and Livestock Show in Birmingham, United Kingdom.

Taken from: Jack Davies and Vickie Robinson, "Farmers Split Over 'Super Dairies'," *Farmers Guardian*, September 17, 2010. www.farmersguardian.com.

While it is true that all farmers benefit from new developments at the top end of the industry, the small farmer has much less capacity to implement such research. He is less likely to hear about new techniques and less able to afford to try them out even if he has. More efficient operations are likely to have staff dedicated to keeping abreast of new ideas.

Prejudice Against Factory Farming Is Misguided

In the United States, for example, most dairy farms are required to develop nutrient management plans to help balance the flow of nutrients and reduce the risks of environmental pollution. These plans encourage producers to monitor feed, forage, animals and fertiliser coming onto the farm and the products, crop, animals, manure and so on leaving the farm. A precision approach to animal feeding results in less overfeeding of nutrients and a subsequent decrease in environmental excretion, such as phosphorus.

In recent years, nutritionists have realised that requirements for phosphorus are much lower than previously thought. These changes have allowed dairy producers to reduce the amount of phosphorus being fed to their cows with a reduction in environmental pollution. Such schemes are more easily implemented on efficient, modern farms. The small farmer is more likely to view schemes such as this as just more bureaucracy, for which he has no time.

The notion that 'cows belong in fields' comes from the same set of ideas that lead supermarkets to put a picture of a farmer on meat packaging. He's leaning on a farm gate surrounded by happy cows, it's summer and the sun is shining. Factory farming conjures images of big business, evil corporations who care only about profits. We need the picture of the farmer to assure us of our ethical righteousness. We are prejudiced against factory farming because of juvenile anthropomorphism. The sentiment behind this prejudice—'Surely cows shouldn't be kept indoors with no natural light for months on end? I'd be miserable if they did that to me!'—is understandable but misguided.

If keeping cows indoors affected their emotional state then it is also likely that milk yields would be affected. Factory farming would not have become the most productive and efficient way of producing milk. Observation of large groups of cows in the US at Central Sands Dairy in Wisconsin has shown that large groups are less affected by social consistency than small ones. In small groups of cows (less than 100), changes in the makeup of the group appears to have a big impact on the cows, and this is shown by a fall in their milk yields as they struggle to adjust to new social orders. In groups of over 200, little impact on milk yield has emerged.

Common diseases that affect cattle are also better prevented in larger herds, the 'closed herd' system acts as a quarantine for diseases which might otherwise be picked up from neighbouring farms or from badgers. Milking machine teats can be decontaminated more systematically to prevent mastitis. Factory farmers are more likely to be able to afford the services of a qualified, registered foot trimmer to prevent lameness, the most common ailment to affect dairy cows.

Prejudice against factory farming needs addressing. Small-scale farming is inefficient and, despite popular belief, no better for animal welfare than larger units. We cannot continue to view the countryside, farmers or livestock in a sentimental way. Large-scale farms like the one still planned for Nocton in Lincolnshire are not as [member of the British Parliament and environmental campaigner] Zac Goldsmith has said "squalid" and "take farming to a new low", rather they are the future of the industry. Without efficient, modern and profitable operations like the one planned for Nocton, farming in the UK faces becoming a lifestyle choice, a hobby, rather than being about feeding the planet.

EVALUATING THE AUTHOR'S ARGUMENTS

In this viewpoint, Jason Smith maintains that animals in factory farms are not exploited. Who has a more convincing argument, Smith or Leah Garces, author of the previous viewpoint? Why? Offer a piece of evidence or quote that swayed you.

Christians Should Avoid Factory-Farmed Products

Charles C. Camosy

"Factory farming... directly contradicts the Bible's understanding of animals."

In the following viewpoint, Charles C. Camosy argues that Christians should avoid factory-farmed products. Factory farming exploits animals, the author contends, and genetically modifies them for economic gain. In addition to its detrimental impact on animals, factory farming, Camosy maintains, harms public health and produces waste that hurts the environment. Christianity insists that humans owe animals kindness, the author asserts, and teaches that it is wrong to cause animals suffering and death without great need.

Charles C. Camosy is an assistant professor of theology at Fordham University in Bronx, New York.

AS YOU READ, CONSIDER THE FOLLOWING QUESTIONS:

1. According to the author, how many chickens are slaughtered each week in the United States?

Most of us are totally disconnected from the process of food production. When taking a bite of pepperoni pizza, we don't think about the fact that we are eating pig. When grabbing a burger, it seldom crosses our minds that we are about to bite into a piece of cow.

As Christians, if someone confronts us with these uncomfortable facts, we justify our behavior by noting that God gave human beings "dominion" over animals in the Genesis creation stories.

But those same stories also insist that God gives us plants to eat, not animals. God creates animals "because it is not good man should be alone." Look it up. Furthermore, both Isaiah and Paul insist that all of creation will be redeemed such that both human and nonhuman animals will live together in a peaceable kingdom of nonviolent companionship.

Humans Owe Animals Kindness

Sadly, that time seems a long ways off. Most of the meat we eat comes from huge corporations via monstrous factory farms, in which more than 100 million chickens are slaughtered each week in the U.S. alone.

FAST FACT

According to the Animal Welfare Institute, cutting off the horns of cattle and removing the beaks of chickens are routine procedures that make it possible to confine these animals in cramped conditions.

The lives of these chickens—like those of most animals in factory farms—are miserable, short and often terribly painful. They spend their pitiful lives in almost complete darkness and in only about one-half of a square foot of living space.

To ensure that they reach full size and move to slaughter quickly, chickens are now genetically altered so that they feel constant hunger and eat as much as they can as quickly as possible. The all-consuming goal of factory farms is to maximize protein-unit output per square foot of space.

The Catechism of the Roman Catholic Church teaches that: 1. It is seriously wrong to cause animals to suffer and die without great need; 2. We owe animals kindness. Those who buy chickens and other animals from factory farms cooperate with a cruel evil and make a mockery of our duty to show animals kindness.

Furthermore, virtually no one needs to eat factory-farmed meat—especially given that we can get more than enough protein from eating relatively cheap lentils, peas, beans and nuts. Eating meat is also one of the major causes of cancer and heart disease; it is hardly surprising that cultures that rarely eat meat have higher life expectancy than those that eat meat regularly.

We also know that the methane produced by the excrement and other bodily emissions of the 50 billion factory-farmed animals killed each year does more to affect climate change than all the emissions of cars and planes combined.

Parishioners of a Detroit-area Catholic church uphold the meatless Friday tenet and enjoy a Friday night fish fry during Lent. Ethical meat-eating is a value that Christians have upheld for centuries.

The greenhouse effect of different diets per person per year, represented as the equivalent in car kilometers

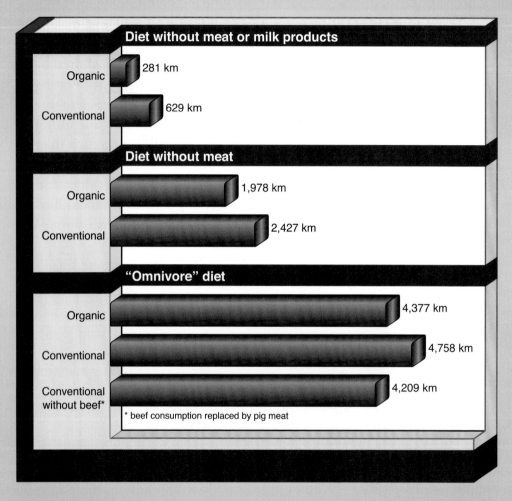

Taken from: "Organic: A Climate Saviour? The Foodwatch Report on the Greenhouse Effect of Conventional and Organic Farming in Germany," Foodwatch, August 2008. www.foodwatch.org.

Protecting God's Creation

The easiest and most productive thing one could do to lower one's carbon footprint—a solemn duty for Christians committed to protect God's creation—is simply to stop eating meat from factory farms.

Interestingly, from the very first Council at Jerusalem, concern about ethical meat-eating has been central for Christianity. The Middle Ages produced St. Francis, perhaps the greatest animal-lover of all time.

Cardinal Joseph Ratzinger, just before he became Pope Benedict XVI, described the issue of factory farming as "very serious" and claimed that "degrading of living creatures to a commodity" directly contradicts the Bible's understanding of animals. Given that his predecessor spoke out about factory farming, might Pope Francis also speak out about it? Given both his namesake and his willingness to try new things, we shouldn't be surprised if he does.

But we need not wait to make good on our obligations to treat animals with kindness and resist the horrifically cruel practice of factory farming. Christians already have a long tradition of refusing to eat meat on holy days.

If full-blown vegetarianism is too intimidating, perhaps we should return to the ancient practice of refusing to eat meat on Fridays and during the holy season of Lent. It would be an important first step toward meeting our serious moral obligations to nonhuman animals.

EVALUATING THE AUTHOR'S ARGUMENTS

In this viewpoint, Charles C. Camosy claims that factory farming degrades animals. How does this factor into his argument that Christians should adopt a plant-based diet?

Factory Farms Have Nothing to Do with Christian Values

Karen Graham

"Why would someone want to bring Christian ideals into the factory farm issue?"

In the following viewpoint, Karen Graham argues that it is misguided to cite Christian ethics to argue against eating meat from factory farms. Her viewpoint is a direct response to the writings of Charles C. Camosy. Graham states that factory farms are money-making enterprises that are not interested in the well-being of animals. She also recognizes that such farms are the result of concentration and industrialization, which have put smaller, family farms out of business. However, Graham derides attempts to use Scripture, specifically passages related to idolatry, to make Christians feel guilty about participating in the consumerism and profit motives evident in factory farming. Furthermore, she argues that such behavior is compatible with Christianity. Graham is *Digital Journal*'s editor-at-large for environmental news.

In his book, *For Love of Animals: Christian Ethics, Consistent Action*, Charles Camosy, an assistant professor of Christian ethics at Fordham University, argues that as a Christian community, we should put as much value on non-human animals as God did when he created the world.

Professor Camosy pushes Christian ethics to the extreme by using factory farming as the basis for his arguments against eating any meats raised by this method. He points out that the animals are mistreated and mishandled, often dying cruel and painful deaths, and all for their idols, consumerism and profits. Camosy says we should bring back the rural family farm because family farms treat their animals with the dignity and respect they are entitled to receive from us.

Factory Farms' Profit Motive

Yes, factory farms are a big money-making industry, with owners looking for a profitable bottom line. The only things on their corporate minds are how much weight they can put on a steer or chicken, and what will it cost them in the amount of feed, pound for pound they will need to purchase. Pollution of streams and water supplies by gargantuan mounds of manure, or how much pain may be inflicted on the animal, be damned.

Factory farms are such a big business that they have taken over whole rural farming communities, driving the small, family owned farms out of business. The competition is just too great. According to Farm Aid, about 330 leave the land every week in this country. Sadly, just two or three corporate farms can replace all those farmers, and make huge profits.

Ethical Reasons for Becoming a Vegetarian

In a 2013 survey, only a small minority of US vegetarians cited religion or spiritual beliefs as their initial reason for becoming vegetarian.

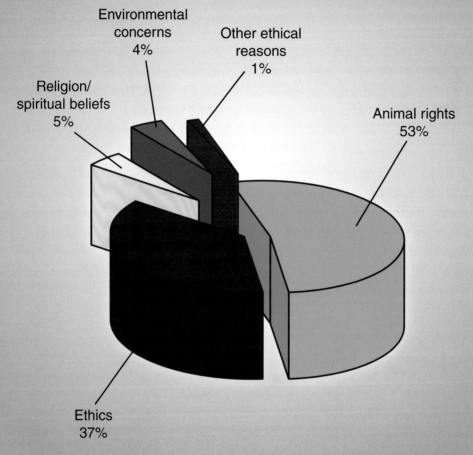

Environmental concerns
4%

Other ethical reasons
1%

Religion/ spiritual beliefs
5%

Animal rights
53%

Ethics
37%

Taken from: Sarah R. Hoffman et al., "Differences Between Health and Ethical Vegetarians," *Appetite*, vol. 65, 2013, pp. 139–144.

Factory farms are the result of the concentration and industrialization of agriculture in America, and they are controlled by an even bigger conglomerate, agribusiness. With the long arm of the federal government and their subsidies, unfair business practices, and questionable contract arrangements, the factory farm is almost untouchable to the public at large. They have so distanced themselves from the consumer that they can proceed to do whatever they want without the fear of public protest.

Consumerism and Profit as False Idols

Camosy enjoins us to avoid eating meat that has been sacrificed to the idols of consumerism and profit. Camosy also wants to make us feel guilty, because man was put over all the animals of the earth, to care for and value them. Instead, he says we don't value them, using them as objects and products to satisfy our desires.

While I am not a bible scholar, I know many verses are often taken out of context, depending on what it is someone wants to get across. Yes, God gave man dominion over all the birds that fly, the fish in the sea, and the animals that walk the earth. As for food, God said, "Every moving thing that liveth shall be meat for you; even as the green herb have I given you all things." (Genesis 9:3)

Professor Camosy writes that "Like the early Christians, we should follow the Biblical mandate to refuse to eat meat that has been sacrificed to our idols of consumerism and profit." But he ignores what the New Testament has to say about idols. In I Corinthians 8:4, it says, "As concerning therefore the eating of those things that are offered in sacrifice unto idols, we know that an idol is nothing in the world, and that there is none other God but one." In other words, there are no idols to a Christian, because there is only one God.

> ## FAST FACT
>
> Technological advances are making farming more efficient, according to the Global Harvest Initiative. For example, tractors that use GPS guidance reduce tillage, fertilizer, seed, fuel, and pesticide inputs by 5 to 10 percent.

We are always hearing that the church and government should not mix, regardless if it's a matter of prayers in school, or "In God We Trust" on our paper money, so why would someone want to bring Christian ideals into the factory farm issue? Factory farming is here to stay. Feeding the world's population cannot be done by Old McDonald anymore.

EVALUATING THE AUTHOR'S ARGUMENTS

In this viewpoint, Karen Graham argues against Charles C. Camosy's belief that eating factory-farmed meat violates Christian ethics. Graham writes that Camosy's argument is based on an obsolete Biblical premise and that supporting factory farming does not violate Christian mandates. Who has a more convincing argument, Graham or Camosy? Explain your answer.

Chapter 3

Is Factory Farming Safe?

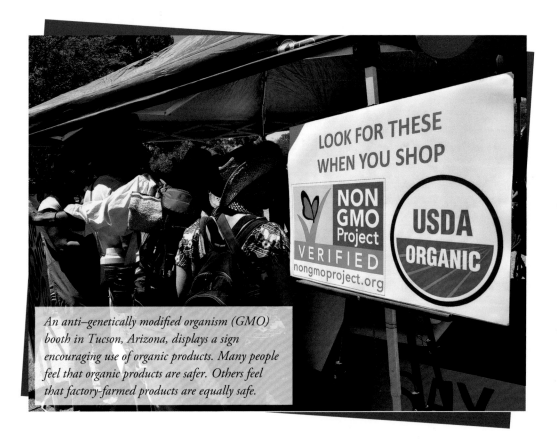

An anti–genetically modified organism (GMO) booth in Tucson, Arizona, displays a sign encouraging use of organic products. Many people feel that organic products are safer. Others feel that factory-farmed products are equally safe.

Factory Fish Farming Is Bad for the Environment

Wenonah Hauter

"Factory fish farms . . . tip the scale towards extreme pollution."

In the following viewpoint from 2011, Wenonah Hauter maintains that factory fish farming is harming the environment. She highlights the dangers of factory fish farming, such as its link to extreme pollution and its detrimental effect on wildlife. The factory fish-farming industry has been mismanaged, Hauter argues, and is modeled after dirty factory farming practices on land. The author encourages the US government to promote low-impact fish-farming systems that are land based and self-contained. Hauter is the executive director of Food & Water Watch, a nonprofit organization that advocates for access to safe food and drinking water.

AS YOU READ, CONSIDER THE FOLLOWING QUESTIONS:

1. According to the author, what results from growing fish in close quarters?
2. How many farmed fish per year does Hauter say could escape unreported as a result of a policy proposed by the US government?

3. The Barack Obama administration proposed to allocate how much money for programs related to factory fish farms in its 2012 budget, according to the author?

I t's not every summer that a fish lands on the cover of *TIME* Magazine. But that's just what happened this July [2011], signaling that the future of our nation's fisheries has become a pressing issue to be seriously debated among the federal government, environmental and consumer groups and of course, fishermen. Unfortunately, this debate was heating up at a time when Congress was mostly focused on issues like the debt ceiling—and right before they left town for congressional summer vacations.

Now that the summer is over, it's time for Congress to weigh in.

The Harmful Effects of Fish Farming

"There's no denying that aquaculture [fish farming] can be messy," the *TIME* story acknowledged. "A badly run near-shore farm of 200,000 salmon can flush nitrogen and phosphorus into the water at levels equal to the sewage from a town of 20,000 people."

Shocking statistics like this are central to the debate on fish farms. True, the world is eating more fish, but farming those fish sustainably to feed our appetite for seafood is no solution. Unfortunately, ocean factory fish farms, like the one mentioned in the magazine piece, tip the scale towards extreme pollution and raise concerns for consumers.

Factory fish farms cram thousands of fish into open net pens and cages. These fish are eating and excreting waste into the sea. Like factory farms on land, growing animals in such close quarters often leads to filth and disease. This necessitates the use of sometimes harmful pesticides, antibiotics and chemicals—toxins which not only flow into the surrounding marine environment, but can also end up on our plates. Moreover, caged fish can escape and overtake or interbreed with wild fish, harming native fish populations.

Unfortunately, the historic mismanagement of our nation's fisheries has left many to wrongly believe that the only way to meet consumer demand is to pack our oceans with these filthy, industrial-scale factory farms. Indeed, this summer, the federal agency charged

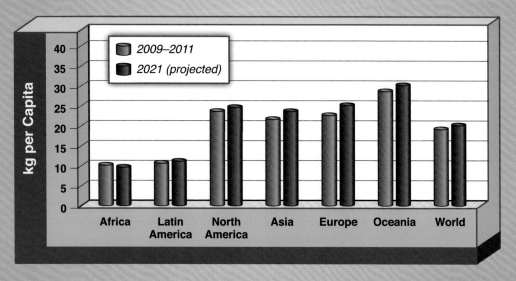

Per Capita Fish Consumption Around the World

Legend:
- 2009–2011
- 2021 (projected)

y-axis: kg per Capita

Categories: Africa, Latin America, North America, Asia, Europe, Oceania, World

Taken from: "The State of World Fisheries and Aquaculture," Food and Agriculture Organization of the United Nations, 2012. www.fao.org.

with regulating our nation's fisheries, the National Oceanic and Atmospheric Administration (NOAA) was busy moving unilaterally to advance this type of fish farming, modeled after dirty factory farming on land.

Stopping the Expansion of Dirty Fish Farms

In June [2011], NOAA and the Commerce Department issued a brand new federal policy calling for more ocean factory fish farming. To add insult to injury, NOAA announced that it would begin moving forward with these farms in the already oil-battered Gulf of Mexico. The government's plan could allow more than 8.6 million farmed fish to escape unreported annually.

Then in July, NOAA awarded the first permit for commercial ocean factory fish farming in the federal waters off the coast of Hawaii, leading my group, Food & Water Watch, to file a lawsuit against the federal agency, as it is questionable whether they even have the authority to issue the permit. If the Hawaiian fish farming company that obtained the permit moves forward with its business venture, no doubt many others like it will rush to scale up operations throughout our waters. NOAA's permit sets a dangerous precedent that allows these fish farming operations to inundate our oceans with pollution, without any real oversight in the future.

Exactly who is behind NOAA's policies towards fish farming? Not consumers, whose valid health concerns are being ignored, and not organizations that are legitimately concerned with our environment or the interests of working fishermen. No, it appears that NOAA's policies cater to the corporations that are pushing big aquaculture to the detriment of us all.

The good news is that fish farming does not have to be dirty. Instead of focusing on the more destructive open ocean farms, NOAA could and should be promoting innovative, low-impact aquaculture systems that are land-based and self-contained.

But NOAA seems to be ignoring this option. In fact, the agency has been pursuing a bigger budget to allow more ocean fish farming. The government has already spent over $44 million in support of the troubled industry. And the [Barack] Obama administration's proposed 2012 budget allocated another $8.4 million for funding programs related to factory fish farming.

Congressional Action to Stop Funding Ocean Fish Farming

It is unfortunate that, at a time when Congress is pushing to trim the federal budget, NOAA continues to request money for this unnecessary, polluting industry—money that could be spent supporting more sustainable industries, job creation and economic growth.

Factory fish farms overcrowd fish into nets or cages. The fish eat and excrete waste in the same area and are exposed to filthy conditions and disease.

Fortunately, Congressman Don Young from Alaska recently introduced a bipartisan bill that would stop federal agencies like NOAA from permitting ocean fish farming until Congress expressly gives them the authority to do so.

This autumn, Congress has an opportunity to put the brakes on these destructive factory farms of the sea. The questions is, will they seize this opportunity by supporting common-sense legislation like Congressman Young's, or will they continue to allow other federal agencies to dictate our fisheries policy on behalf of corporate interests?

EVALUATING THE AUTHOR'S ARGUMENTS

In this viewpoint, Wenonah Hauter claims that the mismanagement of the farmed fish industry is harming the environment. On the basis of what she has argued here, what do you think her reform of this industry would entail?

Factory Fish Farming Is Becoming More Environmentally Friendly

"The majority of farmed salmon [is moving] toward sustainability."

Lindsay Abrams

In the following viewpoint, Lindsay Abrams contends that the factory fish-farming industry is making changes to improve its practices. Although the industry has a bad reputation, the author says, industry-wide reform could transform the future of food production. As seafood consumption rises and the human population continues to grow, wild-caught fish will not be able to feed the world for long, Abrams maintains. The fish-farming industry is moving toward sustainability, the author contends, and soon the consumption of farmed fish will surpass that of wild-caught species. Abrams is an assistant editor at *Salon*.

AS YOU READ, CONSIDER THE FOLLOWING QUESTIONS:

1. As stated by the author, why do farmed fish populations pose a human health risk?

Lindsay Abrams, "The Future of Salmon Is Farming," September 10, 2013. This article first appeared in Salon .com at http://www.Salon.com. An online version remains in the Salon archives. Reprinted with permission.

2. According to Abrams, why did fifteen farmed salmon companies from around the world come together in 2013?
3. What is the fish-farming industry's greatest sin, in the author's opinion?

You know farmed salmon has a bad reputation when even the neo-Nazi meth cooks on "Breaking Bad" look down on it. This week the crew looked to inferior fish to solve a product problem: drugs that were literally a pale imitation of the premium blue stuff.

"Hell, we'll put food coloring in it," they decide. "Like they do farm-raised salmon. I mean, Jesus, do you ever see how pink they make that crap? . . . It sure as hell don't come out the ocean looking like that."

Eating fish responsibly can be confusing. But as even our friends on "Breaking Bad" seem to know, one of the few ironclad rules has been: avoid farmed salmon. Atlantic salmon is always farmed, and farmed fishing is, in the words of Food and Water Watch, "dirty,

Farm-raised Atlantic salmon live in fish cages like these pictured off the coast of New Brunswick, Canada.

unsustainable and inefficient." So don't buy Atlantic. You don't even need a guide to remember that, although Monterey Bay Seafood Watch says:

> Most salmon are farmed in open pens and cages in coastal waters. Waste from these farms is released directly into the ocean. Parasites and diseases from farmed salmon can spread to wild fish swimming near the farms and escaping farmed salmon can harm wild populations. As a result, all salmon farmed in ocean net pens get an "Avoid" ranking.

> Farmed populations also pose a human health risk. They're higher in fat and lower in omega-3's than wild varieties, and may contain high levels of toxins.

The Future of Seafood

"However," the guide continues, "some salmon farmers are making changes to improve their practices." This summer [2013], 15 farmed salmon companies from around the world announced the formation of the Global Salmon Initiative (GSI) to create industry-wide reform. If they succeed, farmed salmon might not only become a good choice—it could be the thing that saves wild fish.

Farmed fish, or aquaculture, is the future of seafood. Very soon, human consumption of farmed fish will surpass that of wild-caught species; as more than one expert I spoke with pointed out, seafood consumption is on the rise, and the human population is still growing. Wild-caught fish won't be able to feed us all for long.

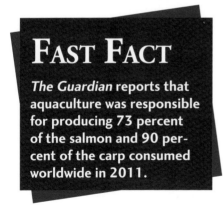

FAST FACT

The Guardian reports that aquaculture was responsible for producing 73 percent of the salmon and 90 percent of the carp consumed worldwide in 2011.

Aquaculture, as it's widely practiced, is easy to vilify as one more thing destroying the environment and depleting natural resources. But despite this bad rap, there's nothing inherently wrong with it. The industry's greatest sin lies in its youth, said Jennifer Dianto Kemmerly,

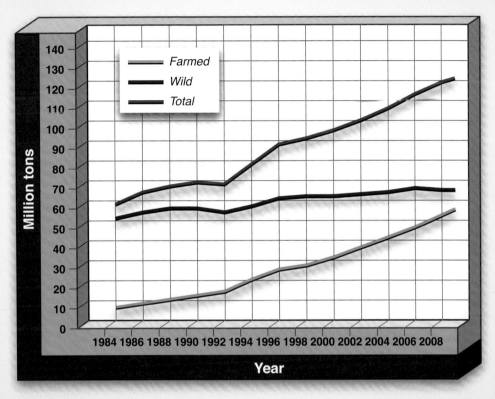

Evolution of World Food Fish Production, 1984–2009

Farmed
Wild
Total

Million tons

1984 1986 1988 1990 1992 1994 1996 1998 2000 2002 2004 2006 2008

Year

Taken from: "Fish to 2030: Prospects for Fisheries and Aquaculture," World Bank Report No. 83177-GLB, December 2013. https://open knowledge.worldbank.org.

director of the Monterey Bay Seafood Watch program. "Fisheries have been going on for thousands and thousands of years," she told me. "Industrial-size aquaculture is just a new industry, and it maybe had some growing pains as it scaled up to meet demand."

Regulations are only starting to catch up. In 2011, the Aquaculture Stewardship Council (ASC) formed and began handing out certifications to sustainable aquaculture operations; salmon will only be the third species eligible for such recognition.

GSI signatories have committed to making 100 percent of their production ASC-certified by 2020. You may not immediately recognize any of their names, but you've probably eaten their product—together, they represent 70 percent of the global farmed salmon industry.

"This is something that probably should have been done 10 years ago," said Alf-Hedge Aarskog. Aarskog is the CEO of Marine Harvest, one of the largest salmon farming companies and a signatory to the GSI. But it's only as the industry has expanded through the world, he explained, that its leaders have recognized how they're all facing the same challenges. "We know that we are all farming fish in the same waters, impacting each other," he said. The industry, in other words, has become mature enough to see the big picture, and to finally address the problems that have been worrying environmentalists for decades.

Already, a small operation unaffiliated with the GSI became the first to receive Monterey Bay's yellow light, or "good alternative" rating. Verlasso is a young fishery that got started in 2006. It was founded, director Scott Nichols explained, in direct response to the environmental problems plaguing bigger aquaculture operations. As such, it got a bit of a head start on reaching a higher standard of sustainability.

Adopting More Sustainable Practices

As the majority of farmed salmon moves toward sustainability, we'll need to amend the way we think of aquaculture. Jason Clay, senior vice president of market transformation for WWF-US, said a lot of what we think we know about the salmon industry—such as the idea that farmed salmon require 10 times more feed than their wild brethren—no longer holds true. The current "farmed is bad, wild is good" mind-set may no longer be productive.

Of course, consumers should be aware that aquaculture isn't yet near where it needs to be. When we spoke about seafood guides, Kerry Coughlin, of the Marine Stewardship Council, reminded me that consumer pressure can push industry toward more sustainable practices.

In one respect, promoting wild-caught salmon lets the industry know that responsibly raised seafood is in demand. The same people who can afford to be picky about not buying clothes produced in sweatshops or produce grown with pesticides may direct their money toward more conscionable fish. But we also need food, period—enough to feed a growing planet. "Two years ago, global aquaculture production surpassed the planet's beef production," said Clay.

For now, aquaculture can still feel like a necessary evil. If you have a choice, it's better to eat wild. But farmed salmon could go from being a problem to being a solution. "We'd like to change people's perception that aquaculture is bad," said Kemmerly. "In fact, aquaculture is necessary."

EVALUATING THE AUTHOR'S ARGUMENTS

In this viewpoint, Lindsay Abrams claims that the fish-farming industry has made significant improvements toward sustainability and that aquaculture is the future of fish production. Do you think the author would agree with Wenonah Hauter that the industry needs more reform? Why or why not?

Factory Farming: Threat to Human Health, Animals, Environment

Rupesh Dutta

"Factory farming can cause the biggest food disaster [for] human beings."

In the following viewpoint, journalist Rupesh Dutta reports on the detrimental effects of industrial meat production. He quotes farm animal advocates who argue that factory farming harms the environment, the animals raised for food, and human health overall. The author describes how factory-farming practices in Jaipur, northern India, risked the animals' well-being in a number of ways, polluted the water and air, and affected the health of people living nearby. Dutta explains that animals raised in factory farms suffer greatly due to crowded conditions, lack of outdoor access, and the inability to express natural behaviors. In addition, animals in factory farms must be fed antibiotics because they live in crowded and unsanitary conditions and have weakened immune systems. Unfortunately, the use of anti-biotics can result in the evolution of drug-resistant bacteria—a great threat to public health. Rupesh Dutta is a writer for IANS, the Indo-Asian News Service, which provides news reports in English and Hindi from India and South Asia.

AS YOU READ, CONSIDER THE FOLLOWING QUESTIONS:
1. What percent of meat globally is produced from factory farming, according to Compassion in World Farming and quoted in the viewpoint?
2. According to Dutta, what does the book *Farmageddon* investigate?
3. What are CAFOs, as defined by Dutta?

Persuaded by the increase and success of factory farms in Brazil during his two-year stay there as a taxi driver, 35-year-old Ajaz Katiyar returned to Jaipur and set up four farms—two for poultry and one each for cows and pig.

Constant increase in the demand for meat and milk in the region kept his business going for over years. But he, like the other factory farm owners in Brazil, ignored proper conditions for the animals.

Keeping thousands of fowls and cows housed in different long and enclosed metal sheds on his property and the overuse of antibiotics to keep the animals insulated from diseases posed a major health risk not just for the animals but also for consumers.

Keeping profit in mind, Katiyar had started using promotants (a medicine) on the animals to induce hormonal changes and mature them early. Also, instead of giving them natural food, Katiyar started giving them grain—a step not at all recommended by the nutrition scientists globally.

Also tens and thousands of animals and fowls in Katiyar's factory farm—a large industrial operation that raises a large number of

FAST FACT

The Food and Agriculture Organization of the United Nations estimates that cattle produce 65 percent of the livestock sector's greenhouse gas emissions.

Estimated Global Emissions from Livestock

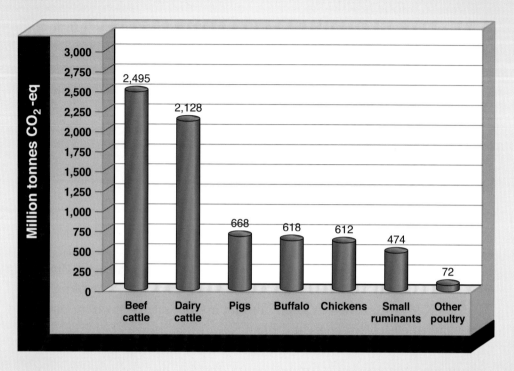

Note: Includes emissions attributed to edible products and to other goods and services from each type of animal.

Taken from: P.J. Gerber et al., "Tackling Climate Change Through Livestock: A Global Assessment of Emissions and Mitigation Opportunities," Food and Agriculture Organization of the United Nations, 2003. www.fao.org.

animals for food—generated millions of tonnes of manure. This was polluting the water and air, and had repercussions on the health of the neighbours and others living nearby.

He and many others who started the same business with profit in mind were later asked by the Jaipur Municipal Corporation (MCD) to either shut their factory farms or shift these to other locations.

Katiyar learned his lesson. He closed down two of his factory farms and is now running the other two by following proper norms.

Philip Lymbery, chief executive of Compassion in World Farming, told IANS that factory farming leads to the proliferation of super bugs.

"Factory farming can cause the biggest food disaster to the human beings that we have not even thought of," he said.

"These unhealthy conditions and additives not only pose threats to the environment and public health, they are also detrimental to the animals themselves. Most factory-farmed hogs and chickens have no access to the outdoors and never see daylight."

As per the Compassion in World Farming, a leading global farm animal welfare organisation, 70 percent of the meat is produced from the factory farming globally.

"Beef cattle and dairy cows spend time outside, but they are crammed onto feedlots with no access to pasture or grass, which is what they are built to eat," said Lymbery, who was recently in India to attend the three-day international conference on "India For Animals" organised by the Federation of Indian Animals Protection Organisation here.

"Lack of outdoor access, inability to express natural behaviours, health problems and stress are caused by production practices, and breeding designed to maximize weight gain or egg and milk production ignoring the animal's welfare," Lymbery told IANS.

He also released a book—*Farmageddon*, an investigative journey on factory farming practices of various nations.

"The stress and unsanitary condition and the direct grain feeding weakens an animal's immune systems, making it more susceptible to infection. Overcrowding allows diseases to spread quickly and easily. Over time, the antibiotics can cause resistant strains of bacteria to evolve."

The Centers for Disease Control (CDC) and the World Health Organization (WHO) had also recently warned against the health risks of concentrated animal feeding operations (CAFOs).

CAFO are agricultural operations where animals are kept and raised in confined situations. CAFOs congregate animals, feed, manure and urine, dead animals, and production operations on a small land area. Feed is brought to the animals rather than the animals grazing or otherwise seeking feed in pastures, fields, or on rangeland.

Nutritional scientist across the globe have highlighted that factory farms across the world are facing tough times. Experts said India and China took up factory farming following the footsteps of Europe and North and South America. But did not follow proper procedures,

An environmental side effect of factory farming is the overloading of nitrogen fertilizer on crops that feed the farm animals. Excess fertilizer eventually ends up in the surrounding waterways causing algae blooms to develop, which are toxic to humans, animals, and fish.

which has led to health problems for both the humans and animals and also played havoc with the environment.

Joyce D'Silva, ambassador for Compassion in World Farming, told IANS that the animals suffer greatly in these farms.

"Despite knowing the fact that the animals, specially cows, give just 13 percent of what they eat, the animals in the farms are fed grain. This changes the food patterns of these animals and they thus suffer from several diseases," she said.

The organisation also states that a third of global grains and 90 percent of soya are used for animals feed, while hundreds of millions of people go hungry.

"Factory farming can lead to rural unemployment and put small-scale farmers out of business, unable to compete," she said. "The animals are also kept in bad conditions, mostly kept in cages, which again affect their health."

EVALUATING THE AUTHOR'S ARGUMENTS

In this viewpoint, Rupesh Dutta argues that factory farming for meat production harms the environment, farm animals, and human health. What alternatives or changes do you think the author would support to address the world's growing demand for meat? Explain.

Viewpoint

4

Factory Farming Spreads Food-Borne Diseases

Michael Greger, as told to Kathy Freston

"We have endangered our health by allowing factory farms to flourish."

In the following viewpoint, Kathy Freston interviews Michael Greger, the director of public health and animal agriculture at the Humane Society of the United States and the author of *Bird Flu: A Virus of Our Own Hatching*. The interview focuses on how factory-farming practices jeopardize the food supply. Greger contends that flu viruses are mutating because of factory farms and that consumers are being exposed to very dangerous bacteria. He also discusses how bacteria and disease spreads within factory farms and contaminates the food supply. He believes that the farming industry must change how it treats animals and put an end to risky practices such as extreme confinement and the nontherapeutic use of antibiotics. Freston is a self-help author of vegan books and a contributor to the *Huffington Post*.

AS YOU READ, CONSIDER THE FOLLOWING QUESTIONS:

1. According to Gregor, what percentage of the meat, dairy, and eggs that consumers eat comes from factory farms?

2. What does Greger say is the source of all food poisoning?
3. What are some of the long-term consequences of ingesting *E. coli*, according to Greger?

After reading *Bird Flu: A Virus of Our Own Hatching*, by Michael Greger, M.D., I was stunned to realize the extent to which we have endangered our health by allowing factory farms to flourish and produce 99% of the meat, dairy, and eggs we eat. Not only are dangerous flu viruses mutating because of these concentrated animal feeding operations (CAFOs), but we are also being exposed to some other very serious bacteria and pathogens. It seems that things have gotten out of hand in our food production, especially in the livestock sector. In my last blog, Dr. Greger explained the growing potential of deadly flu viruses; in Part 2 of the interview, we discuss *E. coli*, *Salmonella* and other worrisome pathogens.

Kathy Freston: Where does E. coli *come from and how does it get into food? Why is it often found on vegetables?*

Michael Greger: *E. coli* is an intestinal pathogen. It only gets in the food if fecal matter gets in the food. Since plants don't have intestines, all *E. coli* infections—in fact all food poisoning—comes from animals. When's the last time you heard of anyone getting Dutch elm disease or a really bad case of aphids? People don't get plant diseases; they get animal diseases. The problem is that because of the number of animals raised today, a billion tons of manure are produced every year in the United States—the weight of 10,000 Nimitz-class aircraft carriers. Dairy cow and pig factories often dump millions of gallons of putrefying waste into massive open-air cesspits, which can leak and contaminate water used to irrigate our crops. That's how a deadly fecal pathogen like *E. coli* O157:H7 can end up contaminating our spinach. So regardless of what we eat, we all need to fight against the expansion of factory farming in our communities, our nation, and around the world.

What percentage of the population gets hit by the bacteria? How many of them die? Could that likely increase?

While *E. coli* O157:H7 remains the leading cause of acute kidney failure in U.S. children, fewer than 100,000 Americans get infected every year, and fewer than 100 die. But millions get infected with other types of *E. coli* that can cause urinary tract infections (UTIs) that can invade the bloodstream and cause an estimated 36,000 deaths annually in the United States.

It seems we only occasionally hear of the very few terrible cases where E. Coli kills; is it really a widespread problem?

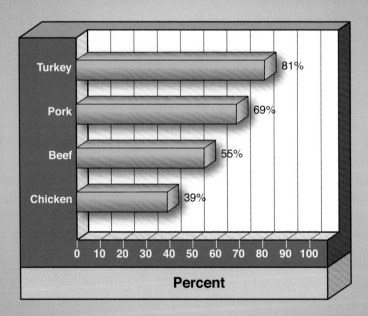

Drug-Resistant Bacteria in Meat Sold in the United States

Percent of meat samples containing antibiotic-resistant *Enterococcus faecalis*

Note: Scientists use *Enterococcus faecalis* on meat as the gauge for fecal contamination and the spread of antibiotic-resistant traits. Calculations made by the Environmental Working Group published in February 2013, based on data from the National Antimicrobial Resistance Monitoring System 2011 Retail Meat Report.

Taken from: Rachel Tepper, "Antibiotic-Resistant Superbugs in Your Meat Are on the Rise: Report," *Huffington Post*, April 16, 2013. www.huffingtonpost.com.

When medical researchers at the University of Minnesota took more than 1,000 food samples from multiple retail markets, they found evidence of fecal contamination in 69% of the pork and beef and 92% of the poultry samples. Nine out of ten chicken carcasses in the store may be contaminated with fecal matter. And half of the poultry samples were contaminated with the UTI-causing *E. coli* bacteria . . . .

Are there any long-term problems for people who ingest E. coli *and have a bad day or two with diarrhea, or is the problem over once out of the system?*

Last month [December 2009] the Center for Foodborne Illness Research & Prevention released a report on the long-term consequences of common causes of food poisoning. Life-long complications of *E. coli* O157:H7 infection include end-stage kidney disease, permanent brain damage, and insulin-dependent diabetes.

Is E. coli *a problem if the meat is cooked?*

With the exception of prions, the infectious agents responsible for mad cow disease and the human equivalent—which can survive even incineration at temperatures hot enough to melt lead—all viral, fungal, and bacterial pathogens in our food supply can be killed by proper cooking. Why then do tens of millions of Americans come down with food poisoning every year? Cross-contamination is thought to account for the bulk of infections. For example, chicken carcasses are so covered in bacteria that researchers at the University of Arizona found more fecal bacteria in the kitchen—on

FAST FACT

The Centers for Disease Control and Prevention estimates that there are 1.3 million cases of *campylobacter* infections each year, 13,000 of which result in hospitalization and 120 in death.

sponges and dish towels, and in the sink drain—than they found swabbing the toilet. In a meat-eater's house it may be safer to lick the rim of the toilet seat than the kitchen countertop, because people aren't preparing chickens in their toilets. Chicken "juice" is essentially raw fecal soup. . . .

The Spread of Infectious Diseases in the Meat Industry

Is factory farmed meat more likely to get E. coli *out into the market, or is all meat (even free range) carrying that potential?*

In chickens, these bacteria cause a disease called colibacillosis, now one of the most significant and widespread infectious diseases in the poultry industry due to the way we now raise these animals. Studies have shown infection risk to be directly linked to overcrowding on factory chicken farms. In caged egg-laying hens, the most significant risk factor for flock infection is hen density per cage. Researchers have calculated that affording just a single quart of additional living space to each hen would be associated with a corresponding 33% drop in the risk of colibacillosis outbreak. This is one of the reasons many efforts to improve the lives of farmed animals is critical not only for animal welfare, but for the health of humans and animals alike.

In terms of other infections like *Campylobacter*, the most common cause of bacterial food poisoning in the United States, *Consumer Reports* is publishing an analysis of retail chicken in their January 2010 issue. The majority of store-brought chickens were contaminated with *Campylobacter*, which can trigger arthritis, heart and blood infections, and a condition called Guillain-Barré syndrome that can leave people permanently disabled and paralyzed. Comparing store brands, 59% of the conventional factory farmed chickens were contaminated, compared to 57% of chickens raised organically. So there might be a marginal difference, but the best strategy may be to avoid meat completely. With the virtual elimination of polio, the most common cause of neuromuscular paralysis in the United States now comes from eating chicken.

What about Salmonella? *Is it really a big deal, or is it just a matter of an upset stomach?*

Salmonella kills more Americans than any other food-borne illness. There is an epidemic of egg-borne food poisoning every year in the

Overcrowding in factory chicken farms is the leading cause of disease among the livestock, which, in turn, can spread to the humans who consume contaminated eggs or poultry.

United States. To this day, more than 100,000 Americans are sickened annually by *Salmonella*-infected eggs. . . .

There are many industrial practices that contribute to the alarming rates of this disease. Most eggs come from hens confined in battery cages, small barren wire enclosures affording these animals less living space than a single sheet of letter-sized paper for virtually their entire 1–2 year lifespan. *Salmonella*-contaminated battery cage operations in the United States confine an average of more than 100,000 hens in a single shed. The massive volume of contaminated airborne fecal dust in such a facility rapidly accelerates the spread of infection.

Factory farming practices also led to the spread of *Salmonella* around the world. Just as the feeding of dead animals to live ones triggered the mad cow crisis, this same practice has also been implicated in the global spread of *Salmonella*. Once egg production wanes, hens may be ground up and rendered into what is called "spent hen meal," and then fed to other hens. More than half of the feed samples for farmed birds containing slaughterplant waste tested by the FDA [Food and Drug Administration] were found contaminated with *Salmonella*. CDC [Centers for Disease Control and Prevention] researchers have estimated that more than 1,000,000 cases of *Salmonella* poisoning in Americans can be directly tied to feed containing animal byproducts. . . .

Would free-range meat or eggs make a difference insofar as preventing it?

There is evidence that eggs from cage-free hens pose less of a threat. In the largest study of its kind (analyzing more than 30,000 samples taken from more than 5,000 operations across two dozen countries in Europe) cage-free barns had about 40% lower odds of harboring the egg-related strain of *Salmonella*. . . .

Finding a Solution to the Spread of Dangerous Bacteria

What is the overall solution to prevent these dangerous pathogens and bacteria?

Over the last few decades new animal-to-human infectious diseases have emerged at an unprecedented rate. According to the World Health Organization, the increasing global demand for animal protein is a key underlying factor.

Swine flu is not the only deadly human disease traced to factory farming practices. The meat industry took natural herbivores like cows and sheep, and turned them into carnivores and cannibals by feeding them slaughterhouse waste, blood, and manure. Then they fed people "downer" animals—too sick to even walk. Now the world has mad cow disease.

In 2005 the world's largest and deadliest outbreak of a pathogen called *Strep. suis* emerged, causing meningitis and deafness in people handling infected pork products. Experts blamed the emergence on factory farming practices. Pig factories in Malaysia birthed the Nipah virus, one of the deadliest of human pathogens, a contagious respiratory disease causing relapsing brain infections and killing 40% of people infected. Its emergence was likewise blamed squarely on factory farming.

The pork industry in the U.S. feeds pigs millions of pounds of human antibiotics every year just to promote growth in such a stressful, unhygienic environment, and now there are these multi-drug resistant bacteria and we as physicians are running out of good antibiotic options. As the UK's chief medical officer put it in his 2009 annual report: "every inappropriate use of antibiotics in agriculture is a potential death warrant for a future patient."

In the short term we need to put an end to the riskiest practices, such as extreme confinement—gestation crates and battery cages—and the nontherapeutic feeding of antibiotics. We have to follow the advice of the American Public Health Association to declare a moratorium on factory farms and eventually phase them out completely. How we treat animals can have global public health implications.

EVALUATING THE AUTHOR'S ARGUMENTS

In this viewpoint, Michael Greger claims that the expansion of factory farms spreads disease. On the basis of his argument, do you think the increase in factory farming is something to be concerned about? Why or why not?

Alternatives to Factory Farming Do Not Prevent Food-Borne Diseases

"Eating organic ... won't necessarily protect you against foodborne illnesses."

Madhu Rajaraman

In the following viewpoint, Madhu Rajaraman contends that local, organic foods are no safer for consumers than nonorganic foods grown on factory farms. The author maintains that the consumption of organic foods does not protect consumers from food-borne illnesses because organics, like conventionally farmed foods, can harbor dangerous bacteria. Although many consumers choose to eat organic to avoid toxins and support local farmers, Rajaraman asserts that there is no scientific research that shows organic foods are less toxic than nonorganic ones. In addition, the author argues, federal organic standards set by the US Department of Agriculture do not include explicit requirements for food safety. Rajaraman was a national fellow at the Food Safety Project in 2011.

AS YOU READ, CONSIDER THE FOLLOWING QUESTIONS:
1. How many people does the author say were infected from eating sprouts from an organic farm in Illinois in 2013?
2. What were the sales of organic food and beverages in 2010, as stated by Rajaraman?
3. According to the author, what are organic labeling standards based on?

Eating organic may limit your exposure to pesticides. It may make you feel environmentally conscious. It can help support local farmers.

But scientists warn it won't necessarily protect you against foodborne illnesses. Organics, like conventionally farmed foods, can harbor dangerous pathogens including *E. coli* and salmonella, News21 reports.

Organic Farming Does Not Prevent Foodborne Illness

A 2006 study in the *Journal of Food Science* did not find a significant difference in the prevalence of *E. coli* between organic and conventional produce. And a 2009 Kansas State University study did not find a difference in the prevalence of *E. coli* between organically and conventionally raised cattle.

Organic foods have caused their share of outbreaks of disease. Last winter [2013], for example, sprouts from an organic farm in Illinois infected at least 140 people in 26 states and the District of Columbia with salmonella. And over a three-month period in 2011, a massive outbreak of a deadly strain of *E. coli* linked to sprouts from an organic farm in Germany killed 50 people and sickened more than 4,300 in several countries.

FAST FACT

The *Food Poisoning Bulletin* reports that Sunland Inc., the largest producer of organic peanut butter in the United States, went bankrupt after a salmonella outbreak in 2012 forced the company to recall many of its products.

Organic products are displayed at a supermarket in London, England. A product's designation as "organic" has no correlation to its level of food safety.

Organics are a big business in the U.S. Sales of organic food and beverages totaled $26.7 billion in 2010, according to the Organic Trade Association, with sales of fruits and vegetables up nearly 12 percent over 2009.

Consumers buy organic for a number of reasons, including to avoid certain pesticides, to encourage smaller farms and to support agriculture that doesn't introduce harsh substances into the environment. In a June 2011 health survey by Thomson Reuters and National Public Radio, 58 percent of respondents said they preferred organic over nonorganic foods. The most popular reasons cited: to avoid toxins and support local farmers.

Despite the public's favorable perceptions, however, "the science doesn't show a difference," said David Lineback, senior fellow in food safety at the Joint Institute for Food Safety and Applied Nutrition at the University of Maryland.

Preference for Organic Foods

Given a choice, would you prefer to eat organic or nonorganic foods?

	Organic	Nonorganic	No Preference
Age			
<35	62.8%	30.5%	6.7%
35–64	60.6%	28.7%	10.7%
65+	44.8%	38.2%	17.0%
Total	**57.6%**	**31.0%**	**11.4%**
Income			
<$25K	56.0%	31.3%	12.7%
$25K–$49.9K	61.2%	31.0%	7.8%
$50K–$99.9K	59.0%	30.0%	11.0%
$100K+	60.8%	26.5%	12.8%
Total	**57.6%**	**31.0%**	**11.4%**
Education			
High School or Less	52.7%	36.4%	10.9%
Some College	54.2%	34.7%	11.0%
College+	63.5%	24.7%	11.9%
Total	**57.6%**	**31.0%**	**11.4%**

Taken from: Thomson Reuters-NPR Health Poll: Organic Food, June 2011. http://healthcare.thomsonreuters.com/npr.

Organic Standards Do Not Address Food Safety

Federal organic standards set by the U.S. Department of Agriculture do not include explicit requirements for food safety, nor are they intended to. The primary purpose of organic farming is not to prevent foodborne illness but to practice and promote environmentally sustainable agriculture.

"We don't purport that organic is healthier than conventional food," said USDA spokeswoman Soo Kim.

"The organic standards do not directly address issues of food safety but instead production and processing and handling methods of agricultural products," Kim said in an email. But, she added, "organic certification by the USDA doesn't preclude any operation from having to meet the food safety and environmental requirements" of two other federal bodies: the U.S. Food and Drug Administration and the Environmental Protection Agency.

Organic labeling standards are based on the percentage of organic ingredients in a product.

For crops, this means growing on land without the application of any prohibited substances (as defined in the Organic Foods Production Act of 1990) and without the use of genetically modified organisms, most conventional pesticides or sewage sludge, for example. Organic livestock must be raised without hormones, fed 100 percent organic feed without byproducts and given year-round access to the outdoors.

Carrie Vaughn, vegetable production manager of the recently certified organic Clagett Farm in Upper Marlboro, Md., said she believes the food safety risks are lower on her farm because of strict standards for manure composting that come with organic certification.

USDA's organic program requires composted manure to be heated to at least 131°F for a minimum of either three or 15 days (depending on the composting system) in order to reduce pathogens.

Distrust of Corporate Agriculture

Vaughn said the close relationship she has with her buyers and their families motivates her to be vigilant about food safety in the field. "It's terrifying for me as a grower to think that I could grow something that could kill a small child," she said. "So we're careful on the farm, and we also work directly with our customers. . . . If something ever happened, it would be so easy to trace that contamination back to us."

Lineback, at JIFSAN, remains skeptical of what he calls consumers' "I-know-the-farmer" attitude. That trust, he said, is rooted not in science but in consumers' feelings about food and a distrust of corporate agriculture.

There is even debate over whether organic food is more nutritious, as proponents maintain. The *American Journal of Clinical Nutrition* reported in 2010 that a study of 50 years of academic articles on the topic found that organic and conventional foods are nutritionally comparable.

So, which is better for you: organic or conventional? In the end, as Lineback noted, "it's a matter of choice and what people believe."

EVALUATING THE AUTHOR'S ARGUMENTS

In this viewpoint, Madhu Rajaraman claims that eating organically farmed foods does not protect consumers against food-borne illness. Given the arguments of Michael Greger in the preceding viewpoint and Rajaraman's in this, which food would you choose to eat: organic or conventionally grown? Why?

Factory Farming Threatens Workers' Health

> *"Plant workers ... are often treated as disposable resources by their employers."*

Southern Poverty Law Center

In the following viewpoint, the Southern Poverty Law Center (SPLC) argues that factory farms exploit their workers and expose them to unsafe working conditions. The organization examines poultry-processing plants in Alabama and concludes that the hazardous environments are putting workers in this industry at risk. Workers face relentless pressure on the mechanized processing line to increase their speed, the author maintains. This pressure has disastrous outcomes, and the organization says that the majority of workers in this industry have suffered from some type of significant work-related injury or illness. The SPLC is a nonprofit civil rights organization that fights for exploited workers, mistreated prison inmates, disabled children, and other victims of discrimination.

AS YOU READ, CONSIDER THE FOLLOWING QUESTIONS:
1. How much poultry do Americans consume each year, according to the author?
2. According to the author, how much higher is the injury rate for poultry-processing workers compared with the rate for all US workers?
3. As stated by the Southern Poverty Law Center, a new regulation by the US government would allow poultry companies to reach what maximum speed on their processing lines?

E very day in Alabama, thousands of people report to work at vast poultry processing plants.

Inside these frigid plants, workers stand almost shoulder-to-shoulder as chicken carcasses zip by on high-speed processing lines. Together, small teams of workers may hang, gut or slice more than 100 birds in a single minute. It's a process they'll repeat for eight hours or more in order to prepare birds for dinner tables and restaurants across America.

This grueling work serves as the foundation of a lucrative industry that supplies the country's most popular meat, a protein source that Americans devour at a rate of more than 50 pounds per person every year.

Alabama produces more than 1 billion broilers per year—ranking it third among states, behind Georgia and Arkansas. It's an industry with an $8.5 billion impact on the state—generating about 75,000 jobs and 10 percent of Alabama's economy—and one that plays a vital economic role in numerous small towns.

But it all comes at a steep price for the low-paid, hourly workers who face the relentless pressure of the mechanized processing line.

A Dangerous Work Environment

Nearly three-quarters of the poultry workers interviewed for this [viewpoint] described suffering some type of significant work-related injury or illness. In spite of many factors that lead to undercounting of injuries in poultry plants, the U.S. Occupational Safety and Health Administration (OSHA) reported an injury rate of 5.9 percent for poultry processing workers in 2010, a rate that is more than 50 percent higher than the 3.8 percent injury rate for all U.S. workers.

Poultry workers often endure debilitating pain in their hands, gnarled fingers, chemical burns, and respiratory problems—tell-tale signs of repetitive motion injuries, such as carpal tunnel syndrome, and other ailments that flourish in these plants.

The processing line that whisks birds through the plant moves at a punishing speed. Over three-quarters of workers said that the speed makes their work more dangerous. It is a predominant factor in the most common type of injuries, called musculoskeletal disorders. But if the line seems to move at a pace designed for machines rather than people, it should come as no surprise. Plant workers, many whom are immigrants, are often treated as disposable resources by their employers. Threats of deportation and firing are frequently used to keep them silent.

Fast Fact

ChangeLab Solutions reported in 2013 that the average life expectancy for migrant and seasonal farmworkers was only forty-nine, compared with seventy-five for the general population.

But workers speaking freely outside of work describe what one called a climate of fear within these plants. It's a world where employees are fired for work-related injuries or even for seeking medical treatment from someone other than the company nurse or doctor. [Workers] describe being discouraged from reporting work-related injuries, enduring constant pain and even choosing to urinate on themselves rather than invite the wrath of a supervisor by leaving the processing line for a restroom break. . . . These workers are among the most vulnerable in America.

A Vulnerable Worker Population

OSHA, which regulates the health and safety of workers in this country, has no set of mandatory guidelines tailored to protect poultry processing workers.

Workers cannot bring a lawsuit to prevent hazardous working conditions or even to respond to an employer's retaliation if they com-

Farming and Fishing Are Among the Most Dangerous Occupations

Occupations with the highest fatal work injury rates, 2013

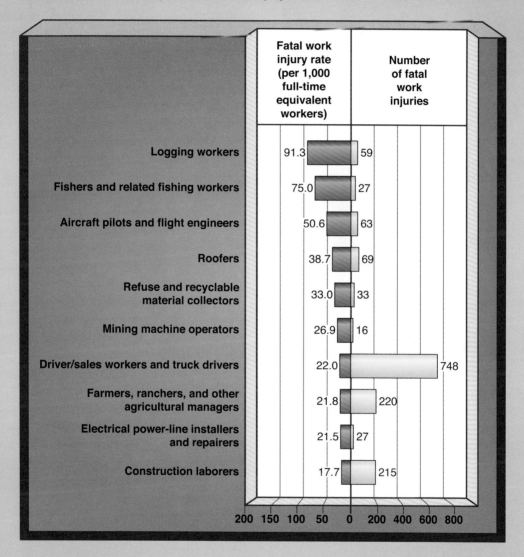

	Fatal work injury rate (per 1,000 full-time equivalent workers)	Number of fatal work injuries
Logging workers	91.3	59
Fishers and related fishing workers	75.0	27
Aircraft pilots and flight engineers	50.6	63
Roofers	38.7	69
Refuse and recyclable material collectors	33.0	33
Mining machine operators	26.9	16
Driver/sales workers and truck drivers	22.0	748
Farmers, ranchers, and other agricultural managers	21.8	220
Electrical power-line installers and repairers	21.5	27
Construction laborers	17.7	215

200 150 100 50 0   200 400 600 800

Note: Data for 2013 are preliminary. Fatal injury rates exclude workers under the age of 16, volunteers, and resident military.

Taken from: "National Census of Fatal Occupational Injuries in 2013 (Preliminary Results)," Bureau of Labor Statistics, US Department of Labor, September 11, 2014. www.bls.gov.

Workers process chicken parts at a Delaware poultry plant. Due to hours of repetitive motion at great speed, poultry workers report a higher than average number of work-related injuries.

plain of safety hazards or other abusive working conditions. Many live in rural areas and have no other way to make a living, which means they must accept the abuse or face economic ruin.

Making matters worse, the U.S. Department of Agriculture is poised to enact a new regulation that will actually allow poultry companies to increase the speed of the processing line—from a maximum of 140 birds per minute to 175. The rule is part of the agency's overhaul of its food safety inspection program, changes that have been harshly criticized by food safety advocates. There is no state or federal line speed regulation designed specifically to protect the safety of workers who produce the food.

This is the face of the modern poultry industry in Alabama—an industry unfettered by serious regulation and blessed with a vulnerable workforce that has lacked a voice in the halls of government and has little power to effect change.

EVALUATING THE AUTHOR'S ARGUMENTS

In this viewpoint, the Southern Poverty Law Center maintains that the poultry industry imposes hazardous working conditions on its employees. Given what you have just read, how do you think the author would reform the poultry industry to make it safer for employees?

Not All Industrial Food Is Evil

Mark Bittman

"Workers in the [food-processing] plants are . . . doing better than they would working in the fields, or in a fast-food joint."

In the following viewpoint, Mark Bittman argues that not all food produced by factory farming is inferior to organic food. The author visits an industrial farm in California to see firsthand how the food is produced. He examines the technology used on the farm and how technological innovations have affected the ability of farmers to supply food for the mass market. He observes safe and clean production lines and concludes that workers on industrial farms such as this one are doing better than those working in other industries. Progress has been made in the factory-farming industry, the author asserts, and contrary to popular belief, "not all industrial food is evil." Bittman is a US food journalist, author, and columnist for the *New York Times*.

AS YOU READ, CONSIDER THE FOLLOWING QUESTIONS:

1. According to the author, what is a harvester?
2. How many acres does Rominger harvest in a twenty-four-hour period, as stated by Bittman?
3. According to the author, what is the average wage at the P.C.P. farm?

I've long wondered how producing a decent ingredient, one that you can buy in any supermarket, really happens. Take canned tomatoes, of which I probably use 100 pounds a year. It costs $2 to $3 a pound to buy hard, tasteless, "fresh" plum tomatoes, but only half that for almost two pounds of canned tomatoes that taste much better. How is that possible?

The answer lies in a process that is almost unimaginable in scope without seeing it firsthand. So, fearing the worst—because we all "know" that organic farming is "good" and industrial farming is "bad"—I headed to the Sacramento Valley in California to see a big tomato operation.

I began by touring Bruce Rominger's farm in Winters. With his brother Rick and as many as 40 employees, Rominger farms around 6,000 acres of tomatoes, wheat, sunflowers, safflower, onions, alfalfa, sheep, rice and more. Unlike many Midwestern farm operations, which grow corn and soy exclusively, here are diversity, crop rotation, cover crops and, for the most part, real food—not crops destined for junk food, animal feed or biofuel. That's a good start.

On an 82-acre field, tomato plants covered the ground for a hundred yards in every direction. Water and fertilizer are supplied through subsoil irrigation—a network of buried tubing—which reduces waste and runoff and assures roughly uniform delivery along the row. (In older, furrow-irrigated fields—in which ditches next to the rows of plants are flooded with water from a central canal—tomatoes at the ends of rows suffer.)

The tomatoes are bred to ripen simultaneously because there is just one harvest. They're also blocky in shape, the better to move along conveyor belts. Hundreds of types of tomatoes are grown for processing, bred for acidity, disease resistance, use, sweetness, wall thickness, ripening date and so on. They're not referred to by cuddly names like "Early Girl" but by number: "BQ 205."

I tasted two; they had a firm, pleasant texture and mild but real flavor, and were better than any tomatoes—even so-called heirlooms—sold in my supermarket.

I mounted the harvester, a 35-foot-long machine that cuts the vine underground and lifts it into its belly, where belts and sensors return dirt, vine, root and green tomatoes to the soil. (All this material is either turned back into the soil or left for sheep to graze on.) Two

The Farmer's Share of the Retail Price of Fresh Tomatoes

Year	Price per Pound		Farm Share
	Retail	Farm	
1992	$1.09	$0.40	41%
1993	$1.08	$0.34	34%
1994	$1.09	$0.28	28%
1995	$1.16	$0.27	26%
1996	$1.21	$0.33	31%
1997	$1.29	$0.35	30%
1998	$1.48	$0.36	27%
1999	$1.37	$0.25	21%
2000	$1.38	$0.31	25%
2001	$1.32	$0.35	29%
2002	$1.32	$0.34	28%
2003	$1.51	$0.37	27%
2004	$1.61	$0.44	30%
2005	$1.61	$0.42	29%
2006	$1.73	$0.41	26%
2007	$1.65	$0.40	27%
2008	$1.74	$0.46	29%
2009	$1.62	$0.46	31%
2010	$1.69	$0.56	37%
2011	$1.67	$0.51	34%
2012	$1.46	$0.35	27%

Note: Calculated by the Economic Research Service, United States Department of Agriculture, using data from the Bureau of Labor Statistics and the National Agricultural Statistics Service.

Taken from: "Price Spreads from Farm to Consumer: Fresh Tomatoes, Field Grown," Economic Research Service, United States Department of Agriculture, November 20, 2013. www.ers.usda.gov.

people on each side sort the continual stream of tomatoes manually before a conveyor transfers the tomatoes by chute to a gondola. When one gondola is full (it holds 25 tons), it's replaced by another. This way, Rominger can harvest around 20 acres in a 24-hour period: 1,000 tons. He estimates his cost at $3,000 per acre and hopes for a $500 profit on each. "Of course," he told me, "sometimes I have a field that collapses on me, and I lose $500."

Fifty years ago, tomatoes were picked by hand, backbreaking piece-work that involved filling and lugging 50-pound boxes. Workers had few rights and suffered much abuse, as did the land: irrigation and fertilizer use were more wasteful, and chemicals were applied liberally and by the calendar, not sparingly by need.

Although the mechanical harvester was controversial when it was first introduced—the United Farm Workers fought its use, fearing it would cost jobs—it revolutionized the industry. (Its impact has been compared to that of the cotton gin.) Yields have more than doubled since the 1960s, and California now produces almost all the canned tomatoes and paste in the United States and more than a third of the world's. For 12 to 14 weeks every summer, Rominger and other growers are harvesting 24/7.

The canneries also operate nonstop. My next visit was to Pacific Coast Producers (P.C.P.), a co-op down the road. It packs for Walmart, Safeway, Kroger, Ralphs and other major chains. Its annual sales, on 20 million cases of whole, diced, crushed, ground and sliced tomatoes; sauce; paste; and more, are more than $250 million.

Imagine all the tomatoes you've ever seen, multiplied by a thou-sand, and you begin to get some idea of the lineup outside P.C.P., which in a 24-hour period may go through 300 gondolas, holding 7,500 tons all together.

At P.C.P., workers first random-sample the tomatoes in an elabo-rate process that determines both where on the processing line the tomatoes wind up (an algorithm decides which fruit from which gon-dolas to combine for the best-tasting sauce, for example) and the exact amount the growers are paid for that load. This year, it's somewhere around 3.5 cents per pound; if you're wondering what percentage of the price of the canned tomato you buy goes to the farmer, I'm figur-ing it's around 2.

The cannery itself is a whirlwind of moist, intense heat and subway-level noise. At peak times, P.C.P. employs more than 1,000 workers. My liberal heart was bleeding at the thought of minimum wage for this tough work—some (not all) of these workstations are as unpleasant as any I've seen—but the plant is unionized. So, according to a P.C.P. spokesman, the average wage is about $17 an hour, and there are benefits.

It's far from paradise, but it isn't hell either. The basic question is this: Are the processes and products healthy, fair, green and affordable?

Workers in the fields have shade, water and breaks; they're not being paid by the piece. Workers in the plants are not getting rich but they're doing better than they would working in the fields, or in a fast-food joint.

Rominger is managing his fields conscientiously and, by today's standards, progressively. He's also juggling an almost unimaginable array of standards set by the state, by P.C.P. and other processors, and even by his customers, who may say things like, "What are you doing about nitrate runoff?"

The canner P.C.P. is running what appear to be safe and clean production lines while producing close-to-"natural" tomato products that nearly anyone can afford.

Oddly, affordability is not the problem; in fact, the tomatoes are too cheap. If they cost more, farmers like Rominger would be more inclined to grow tomatoes organically; to pay his workers better or offer benefits to more of them; to make a better living himself.

But the processed tomato market is international, with increasing pressure from Italy, China and Mexico. California has advantages, but it still must compete on price. Producers also compete with one another, making it tough for even the most principled ones to increase worker pay. To see change, then, all workers, globally, must be paid better, so that the price of tomatoes goes up across the board.

How does this happen? Unionization, or an increase in the minimum wage, or both. No one would argue that canned tomatoes should be too expensive for poor people, but by increasing minimum wage in the fields and elsewhere, we raise standards of living and increase purchasing power.

The issue is paying enough for food so that everything involved in producing it—land, water, energy and labor—is treated well. And since sustainability is a journey, progress is essential. It would be foolish to assert that we're anywhere near the destination, but there is progress—even in those areas appropriately called "industrial."

EVALUATING THE AUTHOR'S ARGUMENTS

In this viewpoint, Mark Bittman claims that some factory farms treat their employees fairly and offer decent working conditions. What policies might the author suggest to improve the working conditions for factory farm employees everywhere?

Facts About Factory Farming

Editor's note: These facts can be used in reports to add credibility when making important points or claims.

Factory Farming of Livestock

According to the United Egg Producers:

- In the United States, 87 percent of egg production is carried out by just sixty-one egg-producing companies that house more than 1 million laying hens each, and sixteen of these companies house more than 5 million hens.
- There were an estimated 283 million egg-laying hens in the United States in a May 2012 census. Of those, only 5.7 percent were cage free.
- Iowa, Ohio, Pennsylvania, and Indiana are the top four states with the most egg-laying hens. In 2012, each of these states was home to more than 20 million laying hens.

According to the *Washington Post*:

- Industrial slaughter facilities that handle cattle can process up to three thousand animals per day.

According to the National Cattlemen's Beef Association:

- The 2014 stock of cattle in the United States was 87.1 million head, down 2 percent from the inventory in 2013, and the lowest since 1951.
- Texas, Nebraska, Kansas, California, and Oklahoma account for more than 50 percent of the total value of sales of cattle and calves in the United States.

According to the US Department of Agriculture:

- Cattle feedlots with one thousand or more head of cattle make up less than 5 percent of the cattle operations in the United

States, but are responsible for marketing 80 to 90 percent of the country's cattle.

- A full 40 percent of cattle marketed in the United States come from concentrated feedlot operations that house and feed thirty-two thousand or more head of cattle.
- As of 2014, the number of hog operations in the United States had declined over the last fifteen years by more than 70 percent as individual farms got larger.
- Large hog farm operations are increasingly specializing in a single phase of the animal's production, rather than raising the animal from birth to slaughter. This fact, along with technological innovations, has contributed to a greater efficiency of scale in the industry.
- Hog operations in the United States are most heavily concentrated in Iowa, Minnesota, and North Carolina.
- More than 43 billion pounds of poultry is produced in the United States each year. At least 80 percent of this is chicken, and most of the remaining is turkey.
- The United States is the world's largest turkey producer, and Americans consume more turkey per capita than anyone else in the world.
- The American Southeast is the leader in broiler chicken (grown for meat) production, led by Georgia, Arkansas, Alabama, Mississippi, and North Carolina.

Factory Farming's Effect on the Environment and Human Health

According to Pew Research:

- Far more antibiotics are sold for animal production than for human health treatment. In 2011, 29.9 million pounds of antibiotics were used for livestock production while just 7.7 million pounds were sold for human health care treatment.
- In 1945, penicillin discoverer Sir Alexander Fleming warned that overuse of antibiotics could lead to widespread antibiotic resistance in bacteria.
- Today, infections of bacteria that are resistant to antibiotics account for twenty-three thousand deaths in the United States

every year and cost the US health care industry $26 million a year.

According to *Consumer Reports*:

- In a test of fresh, whole broiler chickens at grocery stores across the United States, only 34 percent of the meat tested free of salmonella and *Campylobacter*, the two most common bacterial causes of food-borne illness. Sixty-two percent of the broilers tested were contaminated with *Campylobacter*, 14 percent contained salmonella, and 9 percent contained both.
- Of these bacteria, 68 percent of the salmonella and 60 percent of the *Campylobacter* organisms found in the meat proved to be resistant to one or more antibiotics.

According to the Union of Concerned Scientists:

- The manure of animals in concentrated animal feeding operations (CAFOs) is rarely treated by wastewater facilities or septic systems, as is human waste, and is thus more likely to become a source of groundwater contamination.
- Studies of groundwater by the Kansas Geological Survey found that contamination in 42 percent of the wells it tested was a result of animal waste.
- The estimated cost to carry out soil remediation of all the contaminated soil under dairy and hog CAFOs in the United States, a step required to improve groundwater quality in these areas, would be $4.1 billion.

According to the Centers for Disease Control and Prevention:

- A hog farm with eight hundred thousand animals produces 1.6 million tons of manure a year—one and a half times more than the quantity of human waste produced by the city of Philadelphia.
- Livestock in the United States produce somewhere between three and twenty times more manure waste per year than the human population produces.

Factory Farming vs. Small-Scale Agriculture

According to the International Fund for Agricultural Development:

- Globally, small-scale farmers are responsible for producing more than 80 percent of the food consumed in much of the developing world.
- In Africa, 70 percent of the food supply is produced by small-scale farmers.

According to CNN:

- In 2009, 90.5 percent of the farms in the United States recorded sales of less than $249,000 per year. The average net earnings of these farms was only $2,615.
- The top 5.3 percent of all farms took in 73.5 percent of the total farm income in the United States for the same year.
- Only 10.8 percent of farms in the US record sales of $250,000 or more annually, and these farms own 49.4 percent of US farmland, at an average of more than two thousand acres each.

Organizations to Contact

The editors have compiled the following list of organizations concerned with the issues debated in this book. The descriptions are derived from materials provided by the organizations. All have publications or information available for interested readers. The list was compiled on the date of publication of the present volume; the information provided here may change. Be aware that many organizations take several weeks or longer to respond to inquiries, so allow as much time as possible for the receipt of requested materials.

American Council on Science and Health (ACSH)
1995 Broadway, 2nd Floor
New York, NY 10023-5860
(212) 362-7044
e-mail: acsh@acsh.org
website: www.acsh.org

The ACSH provides consumers with scientific evaluations of food and the environment, pointing out both health hazards and benefits. It participates in a variety of government and media events, from television and radio appearances to public debates and forums, and hosts media seminars and press conferences on a variety of public health issues. The council's website features news articles, current research, and multimedia resources.

Cato Institute
1000 Massachusetts Ave. NW
Washington, DC 20001-5403
(202) 842-0200 • fax: (202) 842-3490
e-mail: cato@cato.org
website: www.cato.org

The Cato Institute is a libertarian public policy research foundation dedicated to limiting the role of government and protecting individual liberties. The institute asserts that the concern over the possible health risks of pesticide use in agriculture is overstated. Cato also supports a reduction in the US Department of Agriculture (USDA). The institute believes that the USDA overspends on farm subsidies and that its regulation of many agricultural products keeps food prices high for consumers. The institute publishes the quarterly *Cato Journal*, the bimonthly *Cato Policy Report*, and numerous books and commentaries.

Center for Science in the Public Interest (CSPI)

1220 L Street NW, Suite 300
Washington, DC 20005
(202) 332-9110
e-mail: cspi@cspinet.org
website: www.cspinet.org

The Center for Science in the Public Interest is a nonprofit education and advocacy organization committed to improving the safety and nutritional quality of the US food supply. As a consumer advocate, CSPI fights for policies that promote healthy eating and that prevent food companies from using deceptive marketing practices. The organization is currently campaigning to eliminate junk food from US public schools, eliminate partially hydrogenated oils from the food supply, and require nutrition labeling on the menus of fast-food and other chain restaurants.

Centers for Disease Control and Prevention (CDC)

1600 Clifton Road
Atlanta, GA 30333
(404) 639-3311
website: www.cdc.gov

The CDC is the main health agency of the US government. The mission of the CDC is to promote health and quality of life by preventing and controlling disease, injury, and disability. The CDC provides up-to-date information to the public on health and diseases. The agency publishes several journals, including *Emerging Infectious Diseases* and *Morbidity and Mortality Weekly Report*.

Cornucopia Institute

PO Box 126
Cornucopia, WI 54827
(608) 625-2042

e-mail: cultivate@cornucopia.org
website: www.cornucopia.org

The Cornucopia Institute's mission is to promote economic justice for family-scale farming. It supports educational activities that spread the ecological principles and economic wisdom that underlie sustainable and organic agriculture. Through research and investigations on agricultural issues, the Cornucopia Institute provides information to consumers, family farmers, and the media about organic food and farming.

Environmental Protection Agency (EPA)
Ariel Rios Building
1200 Pennsylvania Ave. NW
Washington, DC 20460
(202) 272-0167
website: www.epa.gov

The EPA is the federal government agency tasked with protecting the environment. The agency regulates pesticides under two major federal statutes. It also establishes maximum legally permissible levels for pesticide residues in food, registers pesticides for use in the United States, and prescribes labeling and other regulatory requirements to prevent unreasonable adverse effects on human and animal health or the environment.

Food & Water Watch
1616 P Street NW, Suite 300
Washington, DC 20036
(202) 683-2500 • fax: (202) 683-2501
website: www.foodandwaterwatch.org

Food & Water Watch is a nonprofit organization that advocates for healthy food as well as access to safe and affordable drinking water. The organization's staff works throughout the country to hold policy makers accountable for the quality of the US food and water supply. Since its creation in 2005, the organization has worked to raise awareness about health concerns and the bottled water industry, to help communities organize against corporate takeovers of public water systems, and to fight for product labeling to ensure consumer safety.

Food First Institute for Food and Development Policy
398 Sixtieth Street
Oakland, CA 94618
(510) 654-4400
website: www.foodfirst.org

Food First is an organization that promotes sustainable agriculture, and it envisions a world in which all people have access to healthy food. Food First is made up of a large network of activists and scholars who produce analyses and educational resources and work closely with grass-roots social movements. Its current projects include the Cuban Organic Agriculture Exchange Program and Californians for Pesticide Reform.

Food Safety Consortium (FSC)
110 Agriculture Building
University of Arkansas
Fayetteville, AR 72701
(501) 575-5647
website: www.uark.edu/depts/fsc

The US Congress established the Food Safety Consortium, consisting of researchers from the University of Arkansas, Iowa State University, and Kansas State University, in 1988 through a special Cooperative State Research Service grant. It conducts extensive investigation into all areas of poultry, beef, and pork production. The consortium publishes a newsletter, as well as an annual report. Available on its website are the consortium's research projects as well as food safety news.

Friends of the Earth (FoE)
1100 Fifteenth Street NW, 11th Floor
Washington, DC 20005
(202) 783-7400
e-mail: foe@foe.org
website: www.foe.org

Friends of the Earth monitors legislation and regulations that affect the environment. The organization uses advocacy campaigns to influence the public, media, and policy makers in order to effect policy change. Its Safer Food, Safer Farms campaign speaks out against the negative impact biotechnology can have on farming, food production, genetic resources, and the environment. The organization has also persuaded grocery stores across the country not to sell genetically engineered salmon. Its website features access to the organization's newsmagazine, blog, annual reports, and fact sheets as well as information about its current campaigns.

Pew Commission on Industrial Farm Animal Production (PCIFAP)

(301) 379-9107
e-mail: info@pcifap.org
website: www.pcifap.org

The commission is a project of the Pew Charitable Trusts and the Johns Hopkins Bloomberg School of Public Health. The PCIFAP was formed to conduct an examination of the farm animal industry. Its commissioners come from various fields, including agriculture, veterinary medicine, public health, government, rural advocacy, and animal welfare. From 2006 to 2008, the commission assessed the agricultural industry's impact on the environment, public health, animal health, and farm communities. Available on its website are a comprehensive report of its findings as well as recommendations for policy makers, members of the agricultural industry, and the general public.

Rodale Institute

611 Siegfriedale Road
Kutztown, PA 19530-9320
(610) 683-1400
e-mail: info@rodaleinst.org
website: www.rodaleinstitute.org

The Rodale Institute was founded in 1947 by organic food pioneer J.I. Rodale. The institute employs soil scientists and a cooperating network of researchers who document how organic farming techniques offer the best solution to global warming and famine. Its website offers information on the longest-running US study comparing organic and conventional farming techniques, which is the basis for Rodale's practical training of thousands of farmers in Africa, Asia, and the Americas.

US Department of Agriculture (USDA)

1400 Independence Ave. SW
Washington, DC 20250

website: www.usda.gov

The USDA is a cabinet-level federal government office charged with regulating agricultural practices and meat production, including organic operations. The USDA has set requirements for the importing and exporting of organic products. More information about this process is available on its website, as well as numerous fact sheets and publications about the state of food in the United States.

US Farmers and Ranchers Alliance (USFRA)

16020 Swingley Ridge Road, Suite 300
Chesterfield, MO 63017
(636) 449-5086 • fax: (636) 449-5051
e-mail: info@fooddialogues.com
website: www.fooddialogues.com

The US Farmers and Ranchers Alliance consists of more than eighty organizations and agricultural partners that work to engage with consumers about how food is grown and raised. The mission of USFRA is to increase confidence and trust in the US agricultural industry. The alliance's website offers resources about food production as well as a multimedia gallery and a blog. USFRA hosts numerous events, including the Food Dialogues, which are designed to bring together industry experts, farmers, ranchers, members of the media, and consumers for panel discussions about food production.

US Food and Drug Administration (FDA)

10903 New Hampshire Ave.
Silver Spring, MD 20903
(888) INFO-FDA (463-6332)
website: www.fda.gov

The FDA is a federal government health agency charged with protecting US consumers by enforcing the Federal Food, Drug, and Cosmetic Act and several related public health laws. To carry out this mandate of consumer protection, the FDA has investigators and inspectors covering the country's almost ninety-five thousand FDA-regulated businesses. Its publications include government documents, reports, fact sheets, and press announcements.

For Further Reading

Books

Eisnitz, Gail A. *Slaughterhouse: The Shocking Story of Greed, Neglect, and Inhumane Treatment Inside the U.S. Meat Industry.* Amherst, NY: Prometheus Books, 2009. The author of this book discusses the changes that have taken place in American slaughterhouses over the last twenty-five years, exploring the impact of deregulation and industry consolidation on worker health, animal welfare, and the consumer.

Foer, Jonathan Safran. *Eating Animals.* New York: Little, Brown, 2009. This book investigates the emotional, ethical, and social considerations that play a role in making dietary choices. Philosophical rumination and scientific inquiry intersect with memoir as the author explores the myths that a society uses to justify its eating habits.

Imhoff, Daniel, ed. *CAFO: The Tragedy of Industrial Animal Factories.* San Rafael, CA: Earth Aware Editions, 2010. With more than 450 photos and thirty essays, this book offers an inside perspective on concentrated animal feeding operations (CAFOs), which ever more frequently are the source of the meat, dairy, eggs, and fish that humans consume.

Kaufman, Frederick. *Bet the Farm: How Food Stopped Being Food.* Hoboken, NJ: Wiley, 2012. The premise for this book is that the food available to consumers is becoming less healthful and tasty even as the industry providing this food gets larger and grows more food than ever before. The author seeks to uncover the reasons for this by investigating the food chain from top to bottom.

Kirby, David. *Animal Factory: The Looming Threat of Industrial Pig, Dairy, and Poultry Farms to Humans and the Environment.* New York: St. Martin's, 2011. This book traces the stories and efforts of three individuals who become advocates for more-sustainable farming methods after large factory farms move into their rural towns. The author complements this narrative with background research on the science, politics, and business of large-scale farming operations.

Leonard, Christopher. *The Meat Racket: The Secret Takeover of America's Food Business*. New York: Simon and Schuster, 2014. Just four companies corner the American market for meat, a fact that has consequences for both farmers and consumers. This book exposes some of the scandals of meat industry consolidation and offers insight into where the system has gone wrong.

Miller, Debra A., ed. *Factory Farming*. Current Controversies. Detroit: Greenhaven Press, 2013. This book explores a variety of viewpoints on industrial agriculture and its relationship to human health and the environment.

Nestle, Marion, and Michael Pollan. *Food Politics: How the Food Industry Influences Nutrition and Health*. Berkeley: University of California Press, 2013. This book exposes the marketing practices of the food industry and its influence on government nutrition policies.

Paarlberg, Robert. *Food Politics: What Everyone Needs to Know*. New York: Oxford University Press, 2010. This book explains the development and interconnection of the global food-production system. The author ties together the many seemingly discordant facets of the global food supply, such as famine and hunger, obesity, international food aid, farm subsidies, and agricultural trade. The book elucidates distinctions between slow food, fast food, organic and local food, and genetically modified organisms, while investigating agriculture's relationship and effect on the environment and food safety.

Periodicals and Internet Sources

Abels, Caroline. "Going Undercover in the American Factory Farm," *Grist*, November 26, 2012. http://grist.org.

Barclay, Eliza. "Industrial Meat Bad, Small Farm Good? It's Not So Simple," National Public Radio, December 17, 2013. www.npr .org.

Braun, David. "Factory Farming Is Not the Best We Have to Offer," *National Geographic*, October 13, 2011.

Cummins, Ronnie. "Why We Need Labels on Food from Factory Farms," Truthout, March 12, 2014. http://truth-out.org.

Damrosch, Barbara. "If Given a Chance, Small-Scale Farms Could Make a Difference in Solving Hunger Problem," *Washington Post,* November 9, 2011.

Datar, Isha. "Why Your Burger Should Be Grown in a Lab," CNN, August 9, 2013. www.cnn.com.

Eng, Monica. "The Costs of Cheap Meat: Critics of Factory Farms Say We Pay a High Price for Low-Cost Food," *Chicago Tribune*, September 24, 2010.

Graham, Karen. "Factory Farms Have Nothing to Do with Christian Values," *Digital Journal*, April 2, 2014. http://digitaljournal.com.

Haspel, Tamar. "Why Farmed Salmon Is Becoming a Viable Alternative to Wild Caught," *Washington Post,* September 23, 2013.

Kenny, Charles. "The Economic Case for Taxing Meat," *Bloomberg Businessweek*, March 31, 2014.

Letheby, Pete. "A Moral Issue Confronts Industrial Farmers," *High Country News*, March 16, 2012.

Lohan, Tara. "How Factory Farms May Be Killing Us," AlterNet, September 17, 2013. www.alternet.org.

McWilliams, James. "The Dangerous Psychology of Factory Farming," *The Atlantic*, August 24, 2011.

Murphy, Dan. "In Praise of Factory Farming," *Dairy Herd Management,* June 22, 2011.

National Public Radio. "How Industrial Farming 'Destroyed' the Tasty Tomato," June 28, 2011. www.npr.org.

Niman, Nicole Hahn. "Support Your Local Slaughterhouse," *New York Times,* March 1, 2014.

Nwanze, Kanayo F. "Smallholders Can Feed the World," International Fund for Agricultural Development, February 2011. www.ifad.org.

Philpott, Tom. "Turkey at $1.38 a Pound Sounds Great. Until You Think About What That Means," *Mother Jones,* November 27, 2013.

Ro, Sam. "Lab-Grown Beef Could End the Food Crisis Before It

Begins," Business Insider, September 20, 2012. www.business insider.com.

Shriver, Adam. "Not Grass-Fed, but at Least Pain-Free," *New York Times*, February 18, 2010.

Walsh, Bryan. "Getting Real About the High Price of Cheap Food," *Time*, August 21, 2009.

Zaitchik, Alexander. "Big Ag's Big Lie: Factory Farms, Your Health and the New Politics of Antibiotics," *Salon*, January 12, 2014. www.salon.com.

Websites

CommonGround (http://findourcommonground.com). CommonGround is a website that promotes dialogue between women from farming families and female consumers. The site provides facts, infographics, and personal narratives about large farming operations in the United States, covering a range of issues, such as food safety, genetic modification, local and organic food, and meat and dairy production.

Factory Farm Map (www.factoryfarmmap.org). Factory Farm Map is an interactive online tool that displays the density and geographic reach of various industrial livestock operations across the United States. The site is a project of Food & Water Watch, which seeks to ensure the safety, accessibility and sustainability of food and water around the globe.

Farmed and Dangerous (www.farmedanddangerous.org). Farmed and Dangerous, a website of the Coastal Alliance for Aquaculture Reform, outlines the environmental problems associated with the salmon farming industry and seeks to promote more sustainable practices in fish farming.

Farm Forward (www.farmforward.com). Farm Forward advocates for more humane and sustainable standards for the animals that are raised for food. Its website provides information about efforts that have been and are being made toward that end.

Stop Factory Farms (www.stopfactoryfarms.org). This website provides a variety of articles about livestock factory farms, specifically divided into sections on beef, poultry, and pork. Stop Factory Farms seeks to inform the public about the real conditions of industrially produced meat.

Sustainable Table (www.sustainabletable.org). This website provides a variety of tools, articles, and links related to sustainable food production and eating sustainably. Resources include guides to key issues in sustainable agriculture, practical tips on recipes for health and nutrition, and ways to promote more sustainable eating.

A Well-Fed World (http://awellfedworld.org). A Well-Fed World seeks to address both human hunger and the suffering of animals used for food by working with grassroots groups in the US and internationally. Its website provides a wealth of information about food production, public health, and the environment.

Index

Picture Credits